CONVERSATION

ADEL
ABDESSEMED

Conversation
with
Pier Luigi Tazzi

Postface
Donatien Grau

ACTES SUD

Adel Abdessemed

Conversation

with Pier Luigi Tazzi

PIER LUIGI TAZZI: There is no reason to be an artist. Of course, a precise role was given once to the figure of the artist in Western culture. At a certain time, it was inscribed in what was, and still is, called the art system. But now things have changed completely, at least since the beginning of the third millennium. Why did you originally choose to be an artist? Why this choice of art?

ADEL ABDESSEMED: I didn't choose art, art chose me. A monk would say that he was "elected."

I was born in Constantine to a Muslim mother in a Jewish house and with Christian nuns as midwives. On that day, I think I brought the gods of monotheism together. My first cry, I see it as the verse of a universal poem, free of borders, color, or country, but tending toward the future.

The first really strong images were those of naked bodies in the hammam. I saw my mother naked, but never my father.

P.L.T.: And so your "election" came very early. Did it go back to your early childhood?

A.A.: Yes, very early. Batna was the crucible of my life. It was in that city that I became familiar with and discovered light, color, sound. The oil lamp, the blue of the sky, the colors of my grandmother's loom, the mud through which I pushed the bottle of gas that was used to make my mother's *galettes*. Batna, for me, was the ululation of the women during the feasts, eating couscous together, the dances, the trances.

Pier Luigi, I'd like to tell you something that happened to me at the School of Fine Arts in Batna. I had to go through a disciplinary hearing; the director and professors assembled to warn me about my "strange laugh." A devilish laugh… I also had my first taste of censorship because of a nude. I constructed myself through fierceness: in disputes, I never hesitated to give headbutts. At the same time, I was already dreaming of sculpture, of modeling clay. I put bottle caps together to make the wheels of a car. With two pieces of cut-out wood, I imagined an airplane. I cut out and made all sorts of accessories and toys for the kids in my neighborhood.

P.L.T.: In the Western cultural tradition, art was often considered a special window to look at or see the world. Was that your perspective, at the beginning?

A.A.: In Algeria, in my country, there were no windows, since houses were the women's world and the street that of men. So the street was my little guide to morality.

That may be why I never hesitated later to use the street as a studio, to be an outlaw. In Western cities, the artist is allowed to use residual lots, he is invited to decorate spaces to be redefined or intervene in housing projects to solve all sorts of problems—as if that could be enough. But when an artist chooses to establish his studio in the public space, he has to ask for permission, pay image rights. That's what I discovered with *Zen*, when I used an outdoor space near my place for the first time… The fact of having had this experience and this street culture on a daily basis in Algeria authorized me, permitted me to authorize myself to use it with ease. I continued in Berlin with *Happiness in Mitte*, *Pressoir, fais-le* then in New York. And then in Paris, I extended the interior space of my studio to the sidewalk of my street to photograph animals, wild animals.

P.L.T.: What do you remember of Algeria, of your childhood?

A.A.: I come from the Aurès mountains, the eastern part, it's dry, full of scars: the land of the Berber Numidians.

I remember silent images, rough landscapes, rocks.

I lived in ignorance as an infant and child in Batna. At that time, without realizing it, I had the experience of not-knowing. At school, teachers were called in from Egypt to teach us Arabic, a language that felt foreign to me at the time; the language of the invaders. It was being crushed by Arabization.

P.L.T.: During the time of your childhood, we had a small house at Al-Hoceima, on the Mediterranean coast of Morocco, where we spent the summer and fall each year. When we arrived in the early 1970s, people spoke Spanish and Chelha, the language of the Berbers that has no written form. When we left in 1978, people were speaking French and Arabic. I've had personal experience with the Arabization of the Maghreb.

A.A.: I grew up in a system that rejected the culture of the land in order to dominate it with fantasies divorced from reality and everyday life. Expression in my country was a rare good, almost non-existent.

My childhood was marked by terror and hatred, the terror caused by war and religions. I experienced the establishment of what was to become fanaticism.

At the time, I had a first shock when my father forbade my mother to speak her own language. Berber was forbidden everywhere, like during the colonial days, when the entire administration used French. Berber came into its own only during feasts, in the songs, because it took on the status of folklore then.

Then the second shock occurred after October 1989, when I was eighteen. My brother asked my mother to stop wearing pants and skirts, and to wear a djellaba instead, because his friends made fun of him. And she did.

My mother was unable to express herself; it was Arabo-Islamism that brought about the degradation of women in our country. Women are persecuted. A kind of apartheid.

P.L.T.: Same thing at Al-Hoceima: in 1970, the girls in miniskirts, and in 1978, more and more chadors.

A.A.: Around 1971-1973, in Batna, where I lived with my family, an illiterate, a war hero, had a lovely little church demolished because it represented Christianity and colonialism. In my family, the Muslim religion was practiced with tolerance. Ramadan, the Eid, I'll never deny that. I consider it a shadow part of myself. After all, I'm a Berber—*Amazigh*—French citizen.

P.L.T.: Sometimes we think an artist becomes an artist when he crosses a line, moves from one path to another, from one direction to another. Was your path in school a straight one, without any detours?

A.A.: I was no good in school—which is why I succeeded.

Luckily for me, I never adhered to the school system. Clearly put, I escaped from the taming of brains which, through idiotic textbooks, assigned pre-established roles to the sexes: Zina in the kitchen and Malik at the market.

The torturer-teachers imported from Egypt never told us that we were beautiful, only that we were dunces.

Art was the only exit for me: a future.

I relied on my instinct and on experience, which were different from those at school.

You know, I was already a man of images then: when I think back on that time in my life, it is images that come to mind, that file past. And of course that must have played a part in my later development.

At the same time, I was an avid reader, avid for philosophy and poetry. I read Nietzsche after curfew—his works were back then forbidden in Algeria—and it had a very strong effect on me. You can well imagine, someone saying "God is dead," that wasn't going to please. I read Victor Hugo, his verses and phrases are still etched in my memory. Like a storm in a skull. Still today, poetry and coincidences play a large role in my work.

What I like a lot about Dvir, my gallerist in Tel Aviv, is that we often talk about the authors we admire so much: Paul Celan and Édouard Glissant, among others.

P.L.T.: Were there things that shocked you so much that you changed your path?

A.A.: For me, Algiers was the city for basic learning: the age of total intoxication and infinite suffering. Living side by side with political assassination, like that of President Boudiaf, and experiencing the expression of the most abject stupidity: the murder of Asselah, director and friend, whose paths often crossed mine at the School of Fine Arts. On the academic side, I discovered abstraction, but the most difficult and important subject for me was alcohol.

In a completely psychotic atmosphere, threatened at every instant of my existence, the only way to survive was to leave a land where you could lose your life at any moment.

P.L.T.: Did your vision of art change a lot when you went from Algeria to Lyon, or do you consider this evolution as the continuation of your trajectory?
A.A.: An acceleration!
P.L.T.: Did you notice a difference between you as a person and as an artist and people who belonged completely to Western culture?
A.A.: I come from the deep wellsprings of the West. Wasn't the West born at Souk Ahras, in Numidia, with Saint Augustine?
I've always been aware of the fact that I possessed a different knowledge, and that the others commanded a knowledge that was different from mine. There is a "canonized" form of knowledge, but there is also this realm of the concrete and of experience, of "not-knowing"—to use Foucault's expression—which corresponds to an *other* knowledge. The main objective was, and still is, to try to merge the two forms of knowledge. My goal is first of all to create oppositions, paradoxes, to put things in crisis, including within my own culture. The next step is to melt everything down and bring it to a crystallization. Very soon I began to think like this by becoming acquainted with other communities, other friends, other histories, other cultures. That particular alchemy was perfect. Difference—I didn't feel it, even if people say that the more specific you become, the more universal you are.
P.L.T.: What did you study at the art school in Batna, then in Algiers, and finally in Lyon?

A.A.: In Batna, and then in Algiers, mostly painting, representational or decorative… When I got to Lyon, more painting, decorative and depressing. It stopped there.
How did I look at the world? Dreaming of changing it.
P.L.T.: And you had quit painting?
A.A.: Well, I never really quit painting, nor drawing. Some of my major references come from the history of painting: scarcely arrived in France, one of my first priorities was to see Grünewald's *Crucifixion* in Colmar, a painting that impressed me enormously: I recently did a fourfold sculpture of it.
But my driving force is struggle… I just finished a series of drawings showing animals attached to explosives. You see, even in drawing, what matters is the struggle, the possibility of an explosion.
At the School of Fine Arts, we learned that paintings had to be hung on the wall and sculpture put on the ground.
I was struck by the amazing German Pavilion taken over by Hans Haacke at the Venice Biennale, *Germania* (1993). The destruction of the marble floor made by the Nazis. In the midst of Germany's reconstruction after the fall of the Berlin Wall, he took history into account.
Only once did I see struggling in painting: it was with Gerhard Richter, in his magnificent *October 18, 1977*, a series of paintings from 1988 about the death of members of the Baader-Meinhof gang at the Stammheim

Prison. There was also something different in painting at the time, something that had nothing to do with this meaning of struggle, but which touched on a profound substance of being, beyond all mundanity, all the dramas of the world, political and social, all contradictions: the art of Palermo, a remarkable painter whom I like enormously, "a flower" according to Joseph Beuys, a last manifestation at the same time as a transcendence of the Romantic concept of the "sublime." Painting, which seems to find an end in Malevich's *Black Square*, seems to extend in Palermo's work to the ineffable beauty of the world, of life in all its material, sensual, and spiritual dimensions.

P.L.T.: What was your feeling when you arrived in Lyon?

A.A.: In Batna, I had met the pastor of Notre-Dame d'Afrique, Father Mariauge. He asked me if I would freshen up the frescoes in the church… I didn't master the technique of fresco painting, so I didn't want to take the risk. To be honest, neither did I want to re-do what already existed. I could have done a new fresco… but he refused. He saw that I was threatened by the climate that was setting in. Upon his advice and that of Sister Colette, I ended up at the poet Henri Le Masne's in Lyon, a city with all violence and exclusion. But a hospitable and refined Lyon. A Lyon discovered and explained by my childhood friend Halim.

The real Lyon was the Lyon of the outsiders. René and Jean-Pierre, a beautiful couple, put me up for two years: they were journalists and had the radio on night and day. I was finding out what was happening in the world. At the Bar de la Détente, I had all my simple pasts.

It was my marriage with Julie, my bliss with her, that led me to love the world and saved me from many catastrophes. Words fail to describe my joy: from the heights of my happiness, I spat down on the petty cares of everyday life.

P.L.T.: Batna, Algiers, Lyon, and after Lyon, Paris, which became "your town," the city in which you decided to live until now.

A.A.: Paris is the capital of desire and renunciation, the eternal home base. I have settled there many times. Paris, that's the promised land. From Paris, I traveled a great deal and became a citizen of the world.

It's the starting point of an intellectual marathon, for intense visits with friends—critics and curators, Hans Ulrich Obrist, Hou Hanru, Guy Tortosa.

With Georges Lapassade, whose dog was drinking from my wine fountain, there was no separation between his place and mine. We had endless discussions. When I was a child, I experimented with trance, and his entire work was a reflection of that. We were made to get along. Even though he was ill and under dialysis, he never tired of our discussions and proximity. Georges had a very firm attitude. He waged an indefatigable struggle against the institutions that make of us what we are not. In passing away, Georges left work in progress behind;

fundamental work to expand our knowledge of the soul.

P.L.T.: In a text that he wrote about you, Georges Lapassade spoke of the "carnal love that is going to change into spiritual love," the "Sufi eros." Did the experience of trance and dispossession play a big part in your conversations?

A.A.: We talked about ecstatic trance, rituals performed in the Algeria of my childhood that came close to "altered states of consciousness." The thing that interested me was upsetting perspectives. Trance permitted you to touch the real, the natural, the truth—depending on how you call it. But you never know where you're going to end up with truth, or how long you can experience it.

P.L.T.: You also lived for long periods in Berlin and New York…

A.A.: New York…

I can get started talking about it only via one artist and one poet: Jackson Pollock and Walt Whitman, both solitary and sublime geniuses. New York is the city of new rhythms, the home of universal brotherhood.

What strikes me every time is the special geometric lines, a prolonged effervescence, a sort of variable tonality. I hung out in Manhattan with a great feeling, and in Queens, near P.S.1, often with Sislej Xhafa, a faithful friend and tireless partner for endless discussions about the art system.

The abolishment of origin, color, and nationality, all that was unimaginable in the Old World.

But then came 9/11, when all the holdovers of differentiation resurfaced. That morning, we were awakened by a call from a friend in Europe, she was in a complete panic. We went outside. There was only one tower left in the distance, burning. From our apartment in the East Village we walked to Houston Street and went downtown a block on West Broadway. Julie had her video camera. And then the second tower fell. In Washington Square, people continued playing chess.

Maurizio Cattelan, who was my neighbor, called me up and we had coffee together. We didn't talk about much.

Scared by the catastrophe and the hate propaganda, I took some time off.

Back in Paris for a few months, Julie was pregnant, we left for Berlin, on the paths of solitude.

Then came the birth of our first daughter, Ksu.

P.L.T.: I remember that when I visited you in Berlin, I tried to introduce you to the art world people that I knew in the city, Italian artists, Scandinavian and German gallerists, etc. But you were always reluctant to make new acquaintances.

A.A.: The artists in Berlin were there only to sleep, because the rents were low.

For me, Berlin was more about music. I loved Hans Scharoun's Philharmonic Hall.

I spent many poetic evenings, evenings of alcohol, with Jimmie Durham, my daughter's godfather, Silvia Ocougne, David Moss.

I love the way that Silvia Ocougne conceives her compositional work, especially her mastery of instrumentals.
Even if her experience comes from the *new music*, she also draws on the ethnic. Style is less important for her than how you think about the creative process.
When I invited Silvia to compose for *God is design*, she went along with my visual idea of three hundred animated ornamental drawings. She recorded thirty-five different improvisations using several *maqâm* (Arabian scales), which were recorded separately, just like I created my drawings separately and put the whole together randomly: she reproduced this in music by creating a very dense texture, which was perfect for me.
P.L.T.: Then you went back to Paris…
A.A.: The City of Paris offered me a studio in the 17th, rue Lemercier, where I produced so many of my works.
Paris then was also the time of special encounters with Douglas Gordon on the one hand, Elisabeth Lebovici on the other, and Caroline Bourgeois who I worked with on the Plateau project. Douglas came one evening and talked about a collaboration. I suggested *One love one god one life*. When I went to England on a student visa, I had to fill out forms in which I was asked what my religions were, one or many, if I was married, once, twice, several times. I was furious, and I just wrote *One love one god one life* on the form. I told this story to Douglas

Gordon and he was stunned, breathless. He took in these words without pretension which, as he said, summed up the world.

He decided to have them written around his neck. He canceled his plane ticket and we went to have it tattooed; he did it without cocaine, that was very hard for him.

Like a manuscript of the world on his body, on the nape of his neck, a sort of perennial relic.

After that I went back to New York as a family and had the great honor of exhibiting and giving courses at MIT, in Cambridge, Massachusetts. There I met Noam Chomsky, Joan Jonas, Jane Farver, Lawrence Weiner, Ute Meta Bauer. I loved the rhythm of life: meeting often at two or three in the morning with student artists.

And then, Pier Luigi, your constant visits, in Paris, Berlin, and as always we discussed quietly, without limits. And each time, these past few years, I dragged you to Aicha's.

P.L.T.: Aicha's bar at the Canal Saint-Martin, the *rai* music in the jukebox, which invites you to to improvise dancing with all the patrons…

A.A.: It's sort of a lost place in the penumbra of the city: neither shadow, nor light, neither day, nor night. For thirty-seven years Aicha has been the owner, she moves at a snail's pace. Her bar stands between water and terra firma, along the Canal Saint-Martin, opposite my studio. Under a diffuse pink and green light, with fluorescent tubes à-la-Dan Flavin, white-collar workers and dark-skinned harragas rub elbows. In the Paris of opulence, Aicha only has sixteen square meters.

Aicha, lost in thought, a blank look on her face, doesn't give a damn about time and laws: behind the bar, a Moroccan woman who lives there illegally; you can smoke there, in her heart she has all the love of the lost souls. Her authority makes her respected, she can get men to speak as well as stones.

It's a place where you can reasonably flee from this gone-crazy world.

P.L.T.: The world has been crazy since the beginning of history. But its craziness changes in the course of time.

When you began to work in art, within the framework of art, it was really the end of a trajectory, that of Western Art, which according to me lasted until the end of the 1980s. From Giotto to the artists of the 1980s, especially European—from Remo Salvadori to Thierry de Cordier, via Franz West, Richard Deacon, Anish Kapoor, Juan Muñoz, Rodney Graham, Thomas Ruff, Jean-Marc Bustamante, to mention only those who are still talked about a lot—there is a sort of linear evolution. An evolution that broke off with British sensationalism, the "Posthuman," the trivial spectacularity of Maurizio Cattelan and company.

A.A.: I was interested at the time in the energy of the generation of "Young British Artists." If we had participated in a project together at the time, it is quite likely that my work and theirs would be put side by side today. It seemed to me back then that I shared with them a similar shift in feeling, beyond all this mannered formalism that characterized the art of the period just before.

P.L.T.: According to me, your work was on an emotive level, much more than on a sensational one. Besides, what had happened between the negative movements of the first half of the 1990s and your appearance on the art scene was the affirmation of an international elite of artists like Rirkrit Tiravanija, Tobias Rehberger, Olafur Eliasson, Carsten Höller, Doug Aitken, Liam Gillick, Superflex, who were about the same age as you.

A.A.: I'm not very familiar with their work or with the whole galaxy of relational aesthetics. In 2004, I thought of inviting them to France to work together on a piece around the "pig soup watered down with Beaujolais" affair, a very violent racist action of the radical right wing. During the winter of 2003, the Bloc Identitaire began organizing soup kitchens in Paris, Nice, and Strasbourg. They served pork there in order to exclude homeless Muslims, as well as Jews.

P.L.T.: In any case, those artists aspired to creating a sort of intellectual elite and you, you had chosen to side with a discriminated social minority.

A.A.: Now that's an intellectual autopsy.

You know that I'm a universal bastard (*laughs*). The problem is not the individual. What matters in the end is the conditions in which a person lives.

P.L.T.: One of the conditions that has always determined the evolution of the person is the economy.

Even in Western Art, at its beginnings between the 12th century—the French cathedrals—and the end of the 13th—Giotto's painting—the resurgence of the cities, the markets, and trade played a decisive role in constructing this model in Europe: that of Western Art. An evolutive, progressivist model that ended up spreading throughout the world, almost in tandem with the model of culture and civilization that bear the same name.

It was economy again at the time of the first industrial revolution and the division of labor that turned art into an activity outside of the general system of production; the system that brought with it what Karl Marx called "alienation." At that time, art constituted an exit from the general system of production. At the same time, it lost its own space and time. A work by Picasso is a mental image, or a luxury object, unlike a fresco by Giotto or a painting by Caravaggio that occupied a particular place. A Picasso did not have a place, except as a luxury object. This created a gap between art and society that still exists today. And it put art objects among those on the market. And again: the first artists who began to occupy a concrete space were the artists of the happenings and Fluxus, as well as the Gutai in Japan. After the American Minimalists, Joseph Beuys, the Italian Arte Povera, Bruce Nauman, Robert Smithson, Eva Hesse, Marcel Broodthaers have established this concrete space for good. The concreteness of this space has principally an economic basis. This was the space of the commercial gallery, of the kunsthalle—museums without collections, of major exhibitions like Documenta and the Biennale, and even the space called alternative art space. And all these spaces were based on economy. When you think that the wood or metal plaques of Carl André, the coal of Kounellis and the faggots of Mario Merz, Beuys's fat, or the empty shells of Broodthaers occupy bourgeois salons and museums, that means that they succeeded in establishing a new economic relationship.

And then, in the 1990s, the economy once again determined a last change. However, it is no longer the economy in general, but that of the market. Someone like Damien Hirst establishes a new relationship with the market economy, not with economy itself.

A.A.: I think that it's probably correct to talk about artists like Kounellis or Joseph Beuys. They invented a relationship to the economy. Jannis Kounellis sold a collector a work with birds: you have to buy birds each time… He also sold a parakeet. Joseph Beuys, olive oil, Giovanni Anselmo, a salad leaf; they invented something, they contributed something. They sold the unsellable, as they say. Artists like Jeff Koons, Damien Hirst, and Maurizio Cattelan did not invent anything in relation to the market: they sold "packages."

The only thing that really matters is what is completely "real." And that's not economics, but art.

P.L.T.: And yet, in a certain way you touch upon the economy in your work.
A.A.: My relationship to the economy boils down to what I do to go bankrupt. I give everything away, I have to spend it all, burn it up.
I behave the way my mother used to when my father got his wages. She'd prepare amazing meals, with meat, pastry. But when the money ran out in the middle of the month, my mother would give us a piece of bread with a drop of olive oil. I always admired the inventiveness that she displayed every time.
One day, I called my mother on the phone and asked her if she would come visit me in France. She said she couldn't talk long because she was preparing boureks and they might burn. Bourek leaves are very fine, made of flour, with meat, potatoes, butter, salt, pepper, parsley, and olives wrapped in them.
Afterwards, she asked me: "Are you alright, my son?" At that moment came the idea of doing *Bourek*, flattening an airplane paper thin and rolling it up to achieve the perfect fusion between airplane and sky. My mother was busy with her role in the family kitchen, and me with the art kitchen. Her family, my art. Like her, if I don't have enough funds for a project, I can still go on making things. Sometimes they cost a lot, and sometimes they don't cost much at all.
A drawing on a piece of paper is enough. As long as it's full of explosive elements, in the literal and figurative sense.

P.L.T.: I think that economy has always been a basic element of art, culture, and human civilization. Animals don't have economies.
A.A.: You know, I take care of the bread that is my substance and food, not the baker.
P.L.T.: Language is another aspect that concerns art directly. When you started working, as I said, there was this tendency toward the positivity of a higher vision offered by intelligence. Among the artists I mentioned, from Rirkrit Tiravanija to Superflex, there was something like an intelligent enjoyment of the world. It wasn't an intuitive, naïve pleasure, it was always a pleasure sophisticated by intelligence.
A.A.: Intelligence and theory are worthless, the only thing that matters is what you actually do.
P.L.T.: And yet it's through language that a relationship to "reality" is established.
In the 1990s, each used a very sophisticated language, all the time. The negative, like Damien Hirst, and the positive, like Rehberger. In the first case, it was the language of tradition. In the second, it was a language renewed, a new language that had to do with a sort of stylistic evolution.
What is your relationship to language? What is your relationship to the new media, your relationship to a certain use of media? In your case, as in the case of other artists of the same generation, there is no recognizable stylistic feature, but rather a similar readiness to use the instruments made accessible by technological progress and linguistic sophistication, which have been put at the disposal of everyone anyway.

A.A.: Style, yes, probably. But that doesn't concern me much. I think it's always up to the others—merchants, connoisseurs, art historians, critics, theoreticians—to establish whether there's a style or not.
And the use that I make of instruments never derives from a particular consideration involving the instrument itself. I use what I find. Language: I never use *Untitled* for my works. Giving a title is naming a reality, making it appear. It's not a matter of summarizing a discourse, but of rendering an image present. The image is what comes to me first. And the title is the transcription of the image.
P.L.T.: John Cage said that technique was never a problem. You use technique in response to an intention.
A.A.: Not necessarily, but it often happens.
P.L.T.: It's as if you found yourself there, with your subjectivity, in your activity as an artist and dancer, and in front of you there was a table with lots of instruments. As if you could pick out exactly the ones that were useful for the expression of your subjectivity, your intention, your idea, your painting. It's not a matter of judging these instruments: they're at the same level as your presence. There's no opposition or distance between your presence and the instruments that happen to be at your disposal.
A.A.: It's relative.
P.L.T.: Then it's you who establishes that there's no distance between you and the instruments you use?

A.A.: It's not at all important to me. In the last analysis, the question is: what's the hardest, the most difficult, the most violent? Death or eternity? What is the reason for my great admiration for the Jewish people? They like the earth, they like objects, they like the present. And, practically, they don't believe in death. They've got that power, attached to the earth.

This love of the present, at the same time as the awareness of its pains, that's what matters more than anything.

P.L.T.: It's not the instant, but the moment, something that has a duration, however brief.

A.A.: I've always been attracted to brevity, which makes it possible to achieve absolute simplicity, like Bach in music. This simplicity is constructed, of course, but it finally has the violence of harmony. It's possible in music, and in the creation of an image.

P.L.T.: In the case of your work, more specifically in the videos, there is often a loop: a limited duration that's going to be repeated, but that's a very precise measure in relation to your idea of time. After which everything explodes and starts all over again. It's something that you can sense, it's perceptible, to a certain extent.

A.A.: The loop, that's the eternal new beginning. And the eternal new beginning, that's speed.

P.L.T.: Speed in your works always seems tied to physical factors.

A.A.: That's true, and in a different way depending on the work. I never repeat myself. There's no repetition in my work without rupture.

Schnell, quick, fast. I was in Berlin and I dropped a camera from a helicopter 700 meters up in the air, because I like the number 7, as you can see in my *Sept frères* or the seven cats in *Happiness in Mitte*. The camera was only knocked out, I recovered the reel undamaged, and I got the effect of the fall, which I made into a loop. What do you see when you experience a quick fall?

That was the heart of this video, which lasts as long as the fall.

The camera went crazy: it had a sort of neurological shock. The object had lived. Life: you add up or subtract images.

The object had exhausted itself, and exhaustion is human. This exhaustion, I also played on it in 1996: I spent several months looking for a flute player who was as old as a father in the Maghreb. This father would play Berber music, the music with which I was rocked to sleep. When I found this father, I filmed him naked to make him lose his identity and keep only the breathing of the flute. But why a man rather than a woman? For me, it is a critique of the "Father" culture. The artist can't always respect his culture; sometimes he has to confront it, create shocks, and spark a revolt. It was one of the most beautiful and overwhelming experiences in making a work (on-camera as well as off-camera), from the beginning of the negotiations to the outcome.

The exhaustion was also a natural one, since he lost his breath. And this natural exhaustion,

I took it up again in *Zen*, an action filmed in a garden.
A white hand pours milk on the black body of Ibou Tal, until the tens of bottles we had are all empty and also until Ibou Tal's physical exhaustion shows under this shower of milk.
Zen deals with the problem of racism and identity in a cosmopolitan city like Paris, one among so many others. A city where there's also tourism, sex, drugs, exile and immigration, illegal aliens, crime, and censorship.
The question for me was: are clandestinity, exile, and immigration utopian perspectives?
Zen signifies the life of our times with a mixture of tenderness, milk, greenery, breathing, and the anger of a man standing up, completely calm.
P.L.T.: This physicality, I find it almost only in your work. It's a contraction of narration, but it's also through this physicality that you manage to express something about time.
A.A.: Speed is the source of eternal new beginnings, the opposite of the repetition of the same. Andy Warhol made wallpaper with the same cow, but he multiplied it. And then the car accidents, the electric chairs, the mushroom clouds are nothing but the compulsive repetition of disasters.
P.L.T.: So time runs in loops. That expresses your sense of time and the decentralization of space. I have the impression that this movement is in opposition to that of the artists of the 1980s, whose work rested on the idea of centrality. A great void, *the sublime void*, and in this void, the

work of art. The work was like a mass, it had its own energy. In your case, I have a completely different impression. The work isn't central. There's no more centrality. At times, it's completely marginal. In the case of the exhibition at the Magasin, works like *Anything can happen when an animal is your cameraman* or *Messieurs les volontaristes* were marginal; not only relative to the physical space of exhibition, but also relative to mental space. The flowering of your work is similar to the flowering of consciousness. It comes to occupy real space then, but no longer has any centrality.

This is much more a feature of your generation—that of Pawel Althamer, Koo Jeong-A, Surasi Kusolwong, Pascale Marthine Tayou, Nari Ward, Yang Fudong, Choi Jeong-Hwa—and of the present generation than of those of the past. And that's why, at this point in our conversation, I'd like to bring in a basic question. What is, for you, the position of the artist today? In the past of the Western culture, there was a sort of progressive linearity that was based on styles, successive movements, in a progressive sequence, having as goal a sort of liberation, an emancipation from previous conditions.

A.A.: This generation opened up a world, I believe. Even so, it chose to go with the world, whereas I chose to face it and change it.

For me, a work doesn't exist if it isn't autobiographical.

Habibi was a self-portrait: my skeleton on a large scale, floating on its stomach in space, as if ejected from the motor of the life-size airplane engine that was behind me. There was at the same time a direct reference to my favorite position for thinking—not the symbolic posture of Giacometti's *Walking Man*, the seated man in Rodin's *Thinker*, or the sacred position of the Buddha. It's a trance, a flight into space, between life and death. I don't deal with the urban landscape but connect with today's skies plowed by civilian and military aircraft.

I represented myself as a skeleton. That's the proof that the work doesn't destroy you. It has a particularity, a space, a time, hidden properties. That's what makes an aesthetic, that's its subject. It doesn't have to prove, it has its own needs, its own dimensions, its own nature.

There's not just the interior that controls the exterior. I think that when you create today, maybe the most striking thing is the disappearance of the artist as myth, as a central figure. This disappearance began with the birth of "curating," because the curators were unable to become writers or chief curators. Originally, they're failed painters.

P.L.T.: It seems to me that the contrast between curators and artists can be described as that which exists between might and power, or between dog and wolf.

A.A.: The curators aspire to a power which they don't have. The artists have a power of a different order, from the humblest to the greatest. Dogs always need a relationship to an other who plays the role of master. Otherwise, they become stray dogs, without tags, or they regress to their original condition as jackals, eaters of garbage and carrion. Wolves, on the other hand, always have the anxiety of the hunt, whether alone or in groups.

The artist is like a hunter, he's in the constant tension of the hunt instead of in relationship with the other.

Dogs bark, wolves howl…

P.L.T.: I think that the figure of the curator is linked especially to the rise of major exhibitions as places for the manifestation of art in the 1960s and to the decline of the function of the museum. When the grand narrative of history started to disappear, the little narratives of the curators were born. Now they constitute an important and indispensable figure in the art system—for better or worse. The competition between the curator and the artist is a false problem. The enemy is another one, inside and outside the system.

A.A.: Pier Luigi, you know that I'm innocent. As for me, I "kill" the curators…

P.L.T.: On the contrary, I think that they're not far from artists, almost of the same family…

For a long time, I've stopped making a distinction between the artist, the artist's ego, even his identity, and "the others," including curators.

For me, they share the same presence, even if I have to recognize that their roles are distinct and different. But I prefer to qualify them as presences rather than as roles.

Similarly, in your work, there's no differentiation between you as a person, as an actor of your own actions and author of your own work, and the animal, in a way. The only distinction maybe—but I'm not sure—is that of consciousness: it is as an author, as an actor/agent, that you are completely conscious of what happens. What does your presence in the work mean, then?

A.A.: I don't think that this phenomenon can be explained. We don't really know anything about it. That's the way it is. I think that the attitude of the artist, whoever he may be, is the most fertile thing today.

But beyond that there's something more secret, which is independent of the control of will. Something that's already there, without our knowing it, that we share and that belongs to us.

P.L.T.: When I see you appear in your own works, photographs and videos, your presence always gives an impression of embarrassment. You're very modest.

A.A.: It's no coincidence that it's my wife Julie who holds the camera. She's present even in my solitude.

P.L.T.: This modesty is the exact opposite of performance. Performance means exhibiting oneself. When you exhibit yourself, on the contrary, one always gets the impression of the awareness of nudity.

A.A.: Every performance has to do with sexuality; you can see it as early as in the Vienna Actionists, Marina Abramović, and the other women of that period. Even Joseph Beuys, when he played the shaman, or Gilbert & George, when they turned themselves into living sculptures. Today there's a confusion between nudity and sexuality. Nudity is the sign of a state beyond the body. It's vaster than sexuality and I see it as an operation of power.

Speaking of nudity, Giorgio Agamben said, "Nothing makes us more poor and less free than the separation from our own powerlessness." The object of art is to act on man's powerlessness and, by acting against the powerlessness that the contemporary world forces on him, to liberate him.

When the king is naked, his power is jeopardized. When Diana is at her bath, when Christ is on the Cross, their nudity expresses powerlessness. That's obviously also what happens in my *Joueur de flûte*. Messouad was naked, shaved, and puffed up with his breath: he looked like a baby. It was a kind of demystification.

P.L.T.: That's interesting, there's always the unveiling of a weakness. When Masaccio depicts Adam and Eve expelled from Paradise, their nudity, their absolute nudity, is not because they have no coats, but because they're naked and it's the moment when they realize the loss of a state of happiness. And this loss reveals their weakness as nudity, or their nudity as weakness, which is practically the same. Happiness appears as a protected condition: the coat of happiness.

A.A.: I've always been interested in the loss of a privileged condition because of a compulsive action.

And at the moment, I'm working on a piece about Zinédine Zidane that I call *Coup de tête*.

P.L.T.: Modesty, a feeling of embarrassment, that's also something that has to do with the situation of art today. And you, as an artist, in a certain way, you're going to appear embarrassed again at being in the world of art.

A.A.: The art world always waits for me with a knife or an ax.

The art world sometimes looks like a castle, but in fact it's a jail.

P.L.T.: I think that there are artists of your generation who have a very naïve relationship with the art world and society in general. They even believe that they can master it. When I am in front of your work, I find that there is always a critical position.

A.A.: Marcel Broodthaers was right: decor is the enemy. Each work has to be able to achieve what I call the "pluperfect." Visually, it has to be so accomplished that it can't help but strike the spectator. Its violence resides in its accomplishment.

When I dealt directly with decor, as in *God is design, Oui*, and *Wall Drawing*, I touched upon several levels at the same time: that of Muslim abstraction against molecular structure in the first of these works; that of the symbolism of the signs of ideological propaganda against the flagrancy/fragrance of a direct experience of matter beyond the visual in the second; and finally, that of Western abstraction against the violence hidden beneath apparently neutral forms in *Wall Drawing*.

The origin of this last work is very peculiar. Marc Blondeau invited me to Cadiz for an exhibition in the south of Spain. The curator explained that all the barbed wire was for the bulls and the Corrida. I replied that I'd never been interested in bulls or barbed wire. But later, walking around in the Tarifa region, I saw Tangier on the other side, and there again barbed wire marking the border. I began to see *Salam Europe* then; a circle five meters in diameter corresponding to sixteen kilometers of barbed wire, which is the distance separating North Africa from Europe. A block of steel, a weight, and at the same time, the porosity of barbed wire.

I read somewhere a sentence in an article about Guantanamo: "To be in the world." It occurred to me that we spend our time constructing and reconstructing our world, our identity. Finding an identity for the work, for me, is the work of a fortune teller. So I rely on my own body to trace a sort of private sphere.

On the contrary, everything produced today is made for consumption and that only makes the decorative depressing.

P.L.T.: You used the same words when you talked about the status of painting that you found in Lyon.

A.A.: Is that so? (*laughs*) Sorry!

P.L.T.: What is a work of art good for?

A.A.: I really don't know, but I'd say it's a kind of solitude.

It brings you back to ecstasy and remains engraved in your mind. Think of my neon sign *Exit*, for example. I played on the signs above exit doors and transformed the term. Exile is positive for me, it's the real way out.

P.L.T.: And for *MohammedKarlpolpot*, wasn't it the same action?

A.A.: God is dead, the devil remains.

P.L.T.: You always assume a presence, while conceptual art for example, which is one of the foundations of all the art being done today, keeps a distance and makes a critical or tautological proposition that in any case, always has something to do with aesthetics.

A.A.: In Harald Szeemann's exhibition *When Attitudes Become Form*, Lawrence Weiner, at that moment, also tried to escape from this prison like a man on death row. It looked as if he had done it with his hands, his nails, to tear the square away from the wall.

It's true that conceptual artists, like the minimalists, re-appropriated the discourse on art, which had eluded the artist's grasp. They were able to do this thanks to a strong progressive political context: the last manifestation of the democratic American utopia in the midst of the Cold War—the Cuban missile crisis, the Vietnam War. But what bothered me about them was their almost overly academic side. The abstraction of knowledge was opposed to a raw violence of desires, which seemed much more channeled and pampered by the Pop movements, ranging from art to music.

P.L.T.: If you wish.

A work like yours is an art of struggle in the political sense of the term. And struggle, conflict, is in the work itself, which is no longer a form of illustration or commentary on this struggle. Nothing to do with propaganda.

In the Western tradition until the first avant-gardes, art could be the expression of a conflict that manifested itself as violence, but this expression was always tied to an agent/author, to his more or less radical stance. In your case, as in that of conceptual art, or even Arte Povera, it's not something tied to an agent/author, to his thinking expressed by his work, it's something that's part of the work itself. Until the avant-gardes, there was a dominant nominalism based on the representation of things: bodies and landscapes, objects and environments, with all the symbolic and narrative meanings. Conceptual art in particular revealed the stakes in nomination: in the compositions of conceptual art you had a thing, an image of the thing and a definition of the thing.

Since then, things are taken as themselves: presented more than represented.

A.A.: The struggle already exists. And we have to continue waging it. The means of struggle are finally all the same to me.

P.L.T.: What is the link, the relationship between spectacle and image? Is there an opposition between these two terms or are they homogenous?

Is the image the objective and permanent result of something that we call spectacle?
A.A.: I'm not going to remake history naively, am I?
Guy Debord's *The Society of the Spectacle* was a great book of the 20th century. Now…
For me, spectacle remains something quite remote. It interests me little as actor/director and even less as spectator.
I have no spectators. On the other hand, I have a public. I don't want to bore it, but I want to help it question its intelligence. The spectator, the man who watches the Gulf War on TV is not my public. I respect my public.
The image is all. And I make no distinction between still and moving images.
The image is vision, total and absolute, a visual condensation of thoughts, emotions, feelings. Seeing, feeling, having an immediate sensory experience. The world penetrates through the eyes into my living substance and nourishes my mind as will and power.
At the beginning of our perceptual life we see things marked by light, we listen to sounds, we feel the mother's warm skin, warmth as the first experience of total happiness. It may be that I haven't evolved much beyond this original condition.
P.L.T.: And the word "action"?
Action, isn't that spectacle?
Spectacle always implies a distance between something active and something passive. The spectacle is something that acts through agents

and is consumed by spectators. In action, there's no distance: action is like a crime in which there's a victim, but no opposition between activity and passivity.

A.A.: Unlike Beuys talking to a dead hare that he considers more intelligent than a live hare, for my part, I explain the sacred to an animal, rather than death. It is the question of how: If you take *Usine*, for example, there's something on the order of a riot, involving numbers, like a collective, group crime. In *Don't trust me*, I talk about the number 1, individual crime. The difference between these two works in which I show death is situated in this question of number. A crime is still a crime.

That makes me think that we find the notion of sacrifice in the three monotheistic religions, the lamb that replaces, is put in the place of man. It can be said that we have always lived in terror.

In *Don't trust me, Birth of love,* or *Usine,* there's no blood because blood disgusts me. They say that these videos are very violent, and yet it's not enough.

P.L.T.: Still in your work there's, on the one hand, a representational aspect: the images. But on the other hand, there are situations that have to do with representation: there is space. Space as the place where you are going to construct the image: the street, the studio, the slaughterhouse, the sea, the air, etc., and as the place of the work's manifestation: the gallery, the museum, exhibition spaces, the collection, etc.

Representation has always been an important factor in art, not just in Western art but in the art of all cultures, all civilizations. What is your relationship to representation? Not only in terms of medium, but in terms of participation, of the articulation of the work. Action and the representation of action.

A.A.: It doesn't reside in taking up something that has already been seen. Like the famous Belgian joke: a Frenchman and a Belgian are watching a cowboy film. The Frenchman bets that the rider is going to fall from his white horse while the Belgian bets that he won't. The cowboy falls. The Frenchman admits that he's already seen the film, and the Belgian admits that he's seen it too. Only he didn't think that the cowboy would fall a second time.

P.L.T.: In the evolution of Western art, there are sometimes non-representational images while the art-representation relationship has always been one of conflict. The introduction of realism into art doesn't contrast with the development of an abstract art. Spectacular horror and physical beauty, the main goals of current iconography, and not just in the realm of art, are they any different from representation as it developed in Western art?

Do you think that representation is still in this tradition of conflict? What is the value of representation in your art and in current art in general?

A.A.: I don't know. When I don't know what to say, it's because I feel like talking in my own language: images.

P.L.T.: You use the mediums of photography and video, which have a correspondence with the idea of representation. Why so often photography and video?
A.A.: That's not true, I use sculpture, the third dimension, not necessarily in relation to place. There's drawing, sometimes texts that I consider as images. Video has something liquid about it, unlike drawing, which is more the result of a crystallization. Drawing is skin: there's an immediate sensuality while that of video is distant. The materials have a life of their own. And images are life itself.
P.L.T.: Today, video and photography are undergoing the obsessive acceleration of technology. Are these developments interesting for you or do you simply pay attention to the tools to the extent that they are coherent with your intention as well as with your notion of representation?
A.A.: No, not even occasionally. I think most of all about things, images…
P.L.T.: Ever since artists have begun occupying a concrete space again, starting in the 1960s, the relationship between the work and space has become more and more important, and in your work, it is basic.
A.A.: If it all functions well, the works crystallize with the space, like in *Double fond et Julie*: there's the mint leaf, the marijuana leaf. Their space is the glass of water. They are not in love, they love each other.
P.L.T.: In all your works there are two levels of reading.

A reading that can be called *lectio facilis*: we see your art as an expression of a gaze upon the world starting from the position/situation of exile, and you as an artist like a virtuous or aggressive representative of post-colonialism.

The other, *lectio difficilis*: the work's power consists of a deep and obscure substance beyond all meaning.

Is it the result of a controlled process or the effect of a poetic construction that doesn't take its possible consequences into account?

A.A.: Actually, I don't know why the spectators of art, these new *célibataires de l'art*—to paraphrase Proust—always refer the artist or the author back to his original background, or the place in which he was born, or his biography. When I like an author, I don't think about his social background or geography, I always leave that out in order to extract from him a pure juice.

I've always been mistrustful of post-colonialism, and not just on moral grounds. It's just something that I reject.

When you experience post-colonialism, it's on yourself, on your body; it's as if you made a soup with poisonous mushrooms, you arrive at the hospital, you're in a coma, you get diagnosed, you get your stomach pumped, then you come out of this violent therapy. You never have this experience again, but that doesn't mean that it won't start again: it's the ultimate in cultural illnesses.

I confess. I was born in 1971, and I've always lived with this idea of a war of liberation. The 1980s, there was a popular uprising and later the civil war, Islam on the march and bloody terrorism. The story isn't finished.

I spent my entire youth in terror and violence. Even if it isn't conscious, it's there.

We're surrounded by all this aggressiveness and violence.

People say that my work is aggressive, violent. My answer to these people is: "I never think about it. I make images…"

P.L.T.: But beyond the violence that's expressed more or less obviously in many of your works, I find that there's something else, something deeper, which I call substance. And if we can easily decrypt violence, this substance remains indiscernible in its power.

A.A.: Beyond the autobiographical experience that ends up in the anecdotal, what interests me is essence. In *MohammedKarlpolpot*, there's an announcement of terror, but there's something else, always above, which is the birth of the work to the point of accomplishment.

This action establishes itself all at once to maintain this immediacy; that's the reason why I never manipulate my images. To maintain the intensity of a cry.

P.L.T.: The titles play a fundamental role in your work, as you've already pointed out. More than expressive or explanatory didascalia—which they sometimes are—they are themselves the subsequent constituents of the work.

What is the relationship between things and words for you?

A.A.: I make no difference between the forest ranger and the woodcutter.

I give titles for myself, to show or trace a line with a scalpel on the body.

But today, in Arabo-Islamic societies, words, speech, and opinion are considered as crimes. This is unparalleled, it's crazy.

P.L.T.: If even words are crimes, what are things? Only the proof of the crime, or some other "thing"?

A.A.: Silence is death. And if you remain silent, you die, and if you talk, you die, so talk and die. I vanish and die in my creation.

When I'm working on *Coup de tête* in a marble block, this gesture produces an effect on the marble, and the marble produces an effect on me. That's the thing.

P.L.T.: That may be the reason why you're always out of the ranks. Every system as such produces ranks, even the art system.

A.A.: As Nietzsche said, "Flee into solitude, my friend."

For me, a work that counts is a cry of solitude.

P.L.T.: I find that one of the most powerful features of art created today throughout the planet is the accent on presence. Not long ago, when I talked to someone about the importance of presence, he told me this little story:

A traveler tired by his long trip sits near a tree that seems to be dry. After a while, the tree starts to bloom. The traveler realizes that this is the manifestation of a presence, a divine presence, if you like. This manifestation is the effect of a presence and not its sign. The effect is more constitutive than the sign, and finally doesn't mean anything. The effect has something to do with substance, the sign with meaning.

I wasn't told the end of this story. Did the traveler continue on his way? Will the tree blossom forever, or will it dry up again?

A.A.: Everyone tells me that the works produced today have a real presence: a real presence in the display cases. Either that, or they don't try to make the public participate in the experience of art. It has to be like fireworks.

P.L.T.: That's obvious in the works of Cai Guo-Qiang.

A.A.: Don't you think that Cai Guo-Qiang's art has faded away since 9/11?

In my work, animals are presences, not symbols, icons, or signs. They're not there to replace something. They're really there.

If there are birds in this tree, it's not a sign: it's because they're there and fight over the flowers and food.

That makes me think of a joke told by Slavoj Žižek that made the rounds in the former German Democratic Republic: There's a German worker who finds a job in Siberia. Realizing that his mail is going to be read by censors, he explains to his friends, "Let's make a code: if you get a letter from me written in normal, blue ink, I'm telling the truth; if it's written in red ink, I'm lying." A month later, his friends receive the first letter, written in blue ink: "Everything's just perfect here, the stores are well stocked, there is plenty of food, the lodgings are spacious and well heated, the movie theaters show Western films, there are plenty of women and they're not very shy—the only thing that's missing is red ink."

P.L.T.: Do we still need red ink in art today?

A.A.: Not necessarily. You know that artists talk about freedom, but they're not free.

That's precisely the depressing sign of the times.

P.L.T.: In the old system of Western culture, and also in other, even different cultural systems, there was a virtuous relationship between life and death, and in this relationship art—not just visual—played a very important and fundamental role.

If we had a lay concept of existence, this relationship would be inscribed within the structural framework of history-culture-civilization; and if we had a spiritualist concept, within the structural framework of faith-religion-spirit.

And now?

Paul Gauguin answered the question, "D'où venons-nous? Que sommes-nous? Où allons-nous?" [Where do we come from? What are we? Where are we going?] with the inscription carved on the doorway of his last house: "Soyez amoureuses, et vous serez heureuses" [Be in love and you'll be happy]. The No Future generation answered with "Sex, drugs, and rock'n'roll."

And now? In the days of Obama and Sarkozy, and all the rest of them, of the post-communist Chinese economy, religious fundamentalism, globalization and the great migrations, of famine and rampant consumerism, little murderous wars and the forecast "collapse" of the planet? What place is left for art? Between its market, its heroes of the day, and its ephemeral *blue chips* on the one hand, and on the other, a vast planetary production of little everyday stories, minority narratives, where to find the lost meaning of enjoyment?

A.A.: At the moment, our societies are sadistic, they harass us in different ways: with stress, fear—we are like animals that spend their time trembling and in fear of being eaten. No use crying. The future is rather bleak.

There's only one life, one death, one mother, one father, who sometimes meet, touch each other, contemplate each other, but who don't know what to do yet.

P.L.T.: *Chto delat?* according to Lenin, and Mario Merz.

A.A.: I'd like to tell you a story that shows that I'm not so optimistic.

A turtle agreed—in spite of its mistrust—to carry a scorpion on its back to join its wife who was waiting on an island. In spite of the scorpion's promises that it wouldn't hurt the turtle, it couldn't help but sting the unfortunate turtle in the middle of the lake.

Just before dying, the turtle asked, "Why do you do that?"

The scorpion answered, "What do you expect, I can't help it, it's in my nature."

P.L.T.: I think I'm much more optimistic than you.

When, at the beginning of the 1990s, the model of Western art reached its end with the last generation of its great artists, from Remo Salvadori to Thierry de Cordier, respectively a peasant and a noble, pulled under by the convergence of the great river of the West with the ocean of the world, there were still signs of life on the Western side. The negatives of British sensationalism—Damien Hirst, etc.—American Posthumanism—Matthew Barney, etc.—spectacular cynicism—Maurizio Cattelan, etc.—or the positive wagers of Tobias Rehberger, Olafur Eliasson, Carsten Höller, etc. But that was obviously the very complete end of the empire.

During the same years, beyond the frontiers of the empire, some new artistic modalities started to break through, to appear on the art scene. They came from far away, from cultures that had nothing to do with European culture: the Japanese, Thai, Chinese cultures. The work is no longer in front of the spectator, but all around (Tadashi Kawamata), aesthetic experience becomes an end in itself and beyond the work (Rirkrit Tiravanija), the work of art exists more as a moment than as a monument (Cai Guo-Qiang), constituting as such the reflection of individual solitude (Hiroshi Sugimoto).

These artists blazed the trails that permitted your generation to assert itself. And I find many features of it in your work, even if they are not directly derived from it. Because art is like an underground river that emerges farther away in more unexpected situations.

A.A.: They are sometimes extraordinary. But they remain distant and ambiguous.

Great geniuses and great neurotics.

P.L.T.: The celebration of the figure of the genius, a being superior to the common mortal, is an invention of the bourgeois culture of industrial capitalism and the neurosis of positivism that was part of the same culture.

But I agree on the distance of artists like the ones I mentioned. In Kawamata's buildings, there are no inhabitants—either they fled, or they're just arriving. In Rirkrit's early works, the artist is never there except as a cook. The works of Cai always refer to a lost community. In Sugimoto's images, there is never a living being.

And what you call ambiguity, I see it as an unlimited opening.

And there, on this sort of empty and waiting inscription tablet, you've begun to inscribe your poems, dense and present.

A.A.: In my opinion, the artists of the 1990s all come from a culture with a capitalist economy. And we have to see in them an art that is monumental and devoid of humor.

P.L.T.: I insist on an indirect derivation, so indirect that it isn't even appropriate to speak of derivation. I mean that the artists who introduced a concept of the work of art different from that of the Western world—the fact that they were all of Asian origin is significant, but not fundamental—prepared the ground on which the now planetary artists of your generation began to inscribe their works. This mark of difference—the introduction of a different aesthetic—is a distinctive feature of your art, an art of difference, difference as multiplicity opposed to the unidirectional linearity of history. Other fundamental factors of the change that took place in the 1990s was the emergence of the feminine sensitivity, with artists like Louise Bourgeois, Marisa Merz, and Marina Abramović, and the proud appearance of subjugated cultures within the framework of art in the U.S.A., which was the center of the art world at the time, as in the case of Jimmie Durham (Native American) and David Hammons (Afro-American).

A.A.: What grips me in the work of these women is a sort of never-ending germination, of expansion without set limits, of fluidity in stark contrast to masculine rigidity, this inevitable flow of energy, from Eva Hesse to Marlene Dumas.

P.L.T.: The later approach that the artists of your generation produced is developing on this ground.

A.A.: Personally, I prefer works based on humor and real experience. Humor is the opposite of parody. It's the expression of the minority in the face of the majority. A manner of preserving the lightness of being. I love the recycled and transient objects of David Hammons, Jimmie Durham, Marisa Merz, Felix González-Torres, Robert Gober, Zoe Leonard, and my friend Sislej Xhafa, who reframe given spaces with their nightmares. They have a substance, and to my mind, they have nothing to do with the monuments and ambiguity of "on site." Their works have a human size and scale to which I am very sensitive.

I was born with the idea that God was already dead. The first man was an artist. In short, there is no logical course.

P.L.T.: Sugimoto once told me that the decadence of the world began with the appearance of the human species.

A.A.: You mean that God is a great artist?

P.L.T.: I have no idea about God except for a figure from mythologies and religious and philosophical doctrines, or representations in art. And so he has nothing to do with art as such. I'm not a believer, you know.

A.A.: I don't believe in rumors either; I believe in my eyes and in my intuitions.

What I like in Sugimoto's pictures, obviously, is the solitude. But he remains egocentric. I don't know him personally but in looking at his work, I can see that he has no ideals, no enemies, no dragons to fight.

P.L.T.: You don't have to. There's already a lot of noise. The visions that you transform into new images charged with meaning or madness pass through your eyes, the ghosts of a future glimpsed pass through your eyes, no longer as a nightmare or the fulfillment of a hope, but as the time of realization itself. It's your nose that smells the mood of the world, the substance of life.

A.A.: Absolutely. That reminds me of one of my trips to Tangier.

Tangier is so sublime that I forgot the purpose of my trip. I was looking for a boat used by clandestine African immigrants to Europe that I wanted to fill with resin sculptures in the shape of black garbage bags and that I wanted to call *Hope* in a direct reference to the sublime painting of Caspar David Friedrich, *Die Gescheiterte Hoffnung* [The Wreck of the Hope]. That also makes me think of the pictures of massacres broadcast on TV. We can almost feel it in our own bodies.

Those are all the effects of brutality.

In 2006, in Berlin, on the night of the World Cup soccer final, Zidane's unprecedented gesture was violent and dark. After a long maturation, I made a sculpture out of it in black marble.

For male society, Zidane's headbutt was a "blow of the ax."

That brutality isn't necessarily in the gesture: it's that of confining codes.

My work *Oui* is an image in the form of an ornamental object, a five-pointed star, in its box, always kept isolated in an empty room.

Beyond its structure, its composition, and material—hashish—I wanted to touch a level different from the visual and cognitive ones that the work of art imposes today, which in this case, is due to the smell. The entire construction of this work is intended to determine an olfactory experience, very subtle, which does not alter the composition but transcends it, displaces it as an aesthetic experience.

A sort of altered state of consciousness; and the ordinary space in which it is exhibited is transformed into a spaced-out state.
Museums reject works that are considered by curators as abnormal.
Art opens up on another world.
Sept frères was a sort of vision like a dream, between dream and nightmare.
The striking thing is the invasion of wild animals in a Parisian street.
There's no explanation...
The only one that you could give is what Freud called the "dream material," the memory of something that happened during the day just before the dream came.
Every time, that engages me in something much more basic, because intuition and visions are closely linked... we possess them, or not... We can have visions that we keep in reserve even if, sometimes, we can't realize them. And for me, each of my works has a relationship to my life. And I always try to achieve absolute simplicity.

P.L.T.: What does commitment mean to you? What is that you call "much more basic"?

A.A.: When we talk about commitment, we always expect a work of art that can topple a regime.
You can topple a state for political reasons and not for poetic reasons... I'm obviously against a lot of things. Artists talk about freedom, but they're not free. I don't work in a factory. My daily life is in my studio.

I'm a father surrounded by his four daughters: there's one on my knees, one moving a book, one tracing arabesques on my drawings or wrinkling them, one flitting by like a bird. It's a souk, and I know that everything comes from that, and I can preserve my cry, my commitment, and my visual challenge.

P.L.T.: Your language is more brief than it is simple, like a syncope in the medical and even phonetic sense of the word.

A.A.: My language is outside of my body.

When the urgent need to do something comes, I do it.

P.L.T.: And that's what you call your visual challenge?

A.A.: Everything is a challenge to me. My life is a challenge, and each work is a challenge and forms a whole in its own right. The work is an action, and actions are challenges.

I consider my commitment as a challenge. The challenge is the result of the fusion of a potential commitment and an application, the construction of the work.

The challenges are not challenges addressed to history or to the future...

If art is seen as an object of history, for me it's more like an action in itself, a presence, an accomplishment.

P.L.T.: *Commitment* on the part of the Self, *challenge* as the modality of a relationship between the Self and everything that is outside of the Self and that surrounds it, *action*, as a reality produced through a constructive process, *presence*, as a reality in itself, independently of the one who produced it, something that's there.

A.A.: Yes, when I speak of experience, there's nothing theoretical about it. To express something that I feel, I greet it like a feeling of bliss and I have to do it.

At the beginning, I control the action, but it escapes me often enough and that's for the best, because it leads me to things that I wouldn't have guessed.

I try to apprehend the essence of a specific instant in a specific place, to realize my work from a drawing, a word, in a natural and direct way. It depends on what I have in mind. And on the urgency.

P.L.T.: Therefore experience against theory, experience as enjoyment, action as an operational practice beyond pre-established controls, touching a substance that can manifest itself as an urgency. All of these characteristics produce a succinct language, a sort of syncope, in which the effect of a blow, collision, *Stoss*—to quote Heidegger—is fundamental.

A.A.: I like to integrate these things as much as possible. And I'm glad that people sense and understand that.

P.L.T.: What importance do you give to the understanding of the others? Experience, enjoyment, action, substance, urgency, *Stoss* are very important terms in your work and more than that, they are on your own "event horizon." And "the people," who are they? What is your relationship and the relationship of your work with them?

A.A.: The action has a form, and the form is communication, in the same way that words have a semantic field and a content. Pleasure, instinct, experience, substance, *Stoss*, in the sense of physical and mental impact, all that is included in the creative urgency, which becomes like a sort of reincarnation. And this reincarnation goes from the action to the exhibition: that's my relationship to human life, to man, to animals, up to the danger that I am in, that we are in. It's a vital necessity: it's my close relationship between thought and the human.

P.L.T.: All that makes me think of the Apocalypse of John, in the etymological sense of the Greek term, which means unveiling, revelation. In the manner of John, the youngest of the Apostles, and probably the author of the book, the artist is in a state of trance and his work is the aesthetic manifestation of a vision, much more than an articulated construction of shapes, and if it is indeed *poiêsis* (*ποιησις*), then in the sense of Martin Heidegger: a moment of ecstasy in which something moves from its stasis to become something else.

But where in the biblical and Christian Apocalypse the prophecies are manifested in a symbolic and mystical form, in art, and in your work in particular, everything is manifested as a direct and immediate vision: sentences, drawings, photographs, video loops, sculptures, manipulated objects, and their placement or staging, rather than installation.

The referential framework is apocalyptically the end of time, especially as the end of historical time, and not as the end of the world and last judgment. It is rather the announcement—"Have no fear," as you already mentioned—of a new time, which is not the day after, the future as the time of plans, but the invisible future in which truth, as you've often said, replaces hope.

And so communication and its forms are not only social instruments to "realize" the conjunction between the intuitive experience of substance and what you call reincarnation.

A.A.: I think that I've managed to reincarnate myself like the Phoenix, or Moses, who led his people to the Promised Land.

And the Last Judgment comes every day, nothing to do with the future, which will be something else, of course.

P.L.T.: Recently, I visited the church of San Vitale in Ravenna for the first time, with the mosaics depicting Justinian, Theodora, and their court. This work marked the end of a world, the Greco-Roman world, already destroyed by Barbarian invasions, and it announced at the same time in an obscure, cryptic way, a world to come without giving any expectations whatsoever: the magic of gold and light, between the reality of the direct experience of a fascination and the conceptual and symbolic meanings concerning political and religious power. After that, more than six centuries went by, the dark and cruel centuries of the European Middle

Ages, before the appearance of a new world, that of European culture and civilization, probably only one of the many possibilities that the announcement in Ravenna pointed to.

In the best work of today, I sometimes have the same feeling, the feeling of the announcement of a world to come, invisible and far away. Will we have to wait as long as before? Will we have to go through the darkness of a new Middle Ages?

A.A.: The question you're asking belongs to the realm of prediction, not of art. I don't think I'm the best person to answer it. All the more as what I do and like, art and poetry, are the opposite of today's consumer society, coming from these horrible governments ruled by money.

Just the same, if I had to give an answer, I would say that we should start with a worldwide strike, like the one I drew. You know that the word drawing in French—*dessin*—is pronounced in the same way as the word for intention—*dessein*. Therefore a drawing is an intention, a design; that is, a way of acting; that is, an impact. Now a drawing is essential in order to define what beauty is. There's no beauty without an impact or convulsion.

Matisse decorated a church, but he wanted to make a museum out of it. People will keep on going to pray in churches, but it's up to us to change what a church is.

P.L.T.: More than a prediction, in many of your works, there's a reaction to the present situation and an announcement of something that is coming. I understand that action has always been decisive in the construction of the work: the work is primarily action for you, much more than reflection, or a mirror. At the same time, aspects of the criticism or the acknowledgement of an end and the power of the change underway are joined in the same work, in the same way that in a living being the combination between life and death is always apparent.

A.A.: I beg those who are going to read us not to consider my works as excuses relative to the past, present, or future...

I wouldn't want to fall into that trap, even if actions like *MohammedKarlpolpot* come across as an announcement, or Zidane's headbutt as an event, or *Bourek* as a trauma, and don't respect history. When history will be respected, tragedy will become a farce, with the melancholic mood of an aftermath. And the artist will play the role of witness in it. To cite Pasolini, whom I love, I don't participate in this cultural genocide: I stay outside. I remain a witness, and that's my struggle—and my commitment; individual, much more than personal, political much more than civic, aesthetic much more than moral, sensual much more than material, aesthetic much more than spiritual.

That's the anxiety of an artist like myself, from a generation that experienced terrorism and that went through the trauma of civil war.

I need elation and poetry.

P.L.T.: The elation of beauty? The poetry of primary emotions?

A.A.: I don't think that we can explain these emotions.

But they produce images. I think of the art and civilization of Ancient Greece, from poetry to tragedy.

The winners of athletic games were glorified by odes from the pens of the most renowned poets and by statues executed by the most famous artists. In fact, Greek sculpture was born as the celebration of youth triumphant in the face of death. Then it evolved toward larger and more common representations like the heroes and the gods, public figures and scholars, poets and philosophers. Monuments from that time on are associated with glory.

The glory of defeats. The glory of the vanquished. Violence. Violence as a reaction. A violent reaction. A violent reaction to bring about a defeat, a loss. When an individual act of violence, as a fitting reaction, brings about a defeat that is not only individual but also that of all those with whom you are joined in the struggle, with them and for them.

Yet my sculpture of Zidane doesn't want to be the monument to a hero. It's the statue of a man as defeated, faced with the enormity of any human defeat. My anxiety is always about knowing how to approach space, I try to develop these possibilities in relation to what I need, for Zidane offered us Materazzi's elation. I find this gift incredibly exhilarating.

P.L.T.: So beauty is always connected with death for you? The monument with defeat?

Materazzi exalted by what?

A.A.: For me, beauty is not a protest, but a proclamation. A sort of unique event.

It's an exultation that remains without a response.

How to make a sculpture without falling into the trap of justifying myself for benefiting from Materazzi's drama: that's the challenge to be taken up. I prefer to maintain the emotion. But not the emotions of the screen.

The title *Coup de tête* is self-explanatory.

You know that sports today have largely surpassed religion and the arts... although it's not even the most exacting model of performance... It must be said that the sportsman, like the politician, or the fashion models, or any person involved in the performance that is fashion, embodies the ideal type of modern man, an ideal that consists in constantly changing.

It's a sort of chameleon, transvestite, refined strategist, who constantly stages himself.

It's no longer fiction that takes its inspiration from reality, but reality that surpasses fiction. No matter.

P.L.T.: What meaning do you give to the vicious relationship between the performance of the spectacle—especially in the media—and power, real and fictional?

A.A.: Power is vicious. Everything is a simulacrum. Politics as reality TV. The one is no more real than the other since the relationship that you have with the spectacle of politics, with its simulacrum, is exactly the same as when you look at the actors in *Loft Story*. You ask yourself all the time how the participants are going to interact, like in a zoo, a cage with a screen. That's what I tried to deal with in my drawing series *La Grande Parade*.

I call these animals the "Petites Gens."

P.L.T.: "Petites Gens" is a name that refers to the Little People described by James Frazer in *The Golden Bough*, a fantastic procession of fairies, will-o'-the-wisps, elves, genies, demons, that inhabit the folklore of all the cultures in the world, and that recently reappeared in Murakami Haruki's latest novel, *IQ84*.

A.A.: You're right in stressing the importance of the myth of the golden bough discussed by James Frazer, a magnificent myth that we can never read often enough. He reported so many stories without ever leaving the place where he lived. It's fascinating.

Frazer combines many myths, sources drawn from oral literature. These tales are very rich in creatures, figures, monsters, and they recall the Kabyle tales collected by Frobenius, which I often read to my children. I love fables and ancestral folktales.

My animals in *La Grande Parade* are invisible kamikazes—and in the minority.

The "Little People" are the power of the minorities.

According to Arabian texts from many different periods, this "tribe" lived in the "northernmost" place. But where is this North situated? At that time, the North wasn't the one we know today.

It was situated in the Orient, the cradle of civilization: between the Himalayas and the Urals, according to Ibn Khaldoun and a large number of other historians and geographers. The Gogs and Magogs were very numerous. Their morphology has been variously described: for some, they were dwarves, for others, giants, and for the more rational, normal people.

We know nothing of their civilization and no one has ever reported any concrete information, except that they were described as barbarian and unruly.

P.L.T.: The Gogs and Magogs are the perfect symbol for a devastating and destructive horde, final and without recourse: the end of the world of human beings. It's not even said that they'll survive themselves to reconstruct an equivalent, or its opposite!

A.A.: During the Persian Gulf war, this story cropped up in the middle of every conversation, and people really believed in this myth. I heard that Jacques Chirac's advisors once called a Swiss professor to find out more about the Gogs and Magogs. George Bush is supposed to have said that they were the forces at work in the Middle East.

They are the cliché and scarecrow brandished by the religious and political chief as an ultimate weapon to terrify subjects unwilling to follow the "indicated direction"!

They exist only as a reminder of terror and that's what their name is forever associated with. This myth talks about a people without a past, but endowed with a "Great Future"! Their coming appearance or their return will be a sure mark and a first sign of the end of the world. What remains constant in each version is the role played by a wall. Dhû-l-Qarnayn, in an expedition to the Northeast, encountered a peaceful people who complained of the ravages caused by their barbarian and warlike neighbors, the Gogs and Magogs. They promised him riches and recognition if he would help get rid of them.

Being an enlightened builder, he erected between two mountains a wall of iron blocks which he coated with molten copper. In this way he was able to foil the attacks of the Gogs and Magogs, who were unable to climb over or breach it. This is like the myth of the golden bough: the only thing missing is the Tree of God.

P.L.T.: This symbol of the wall has a contemporary resonance.

A.A.: It's easy to find parallels. The wall moves from place to place: from Berlin it moved to Israel.

When I was in Berlin, there were remains of the wall. In Israel, each time I went there, I saw it being built.

These myths are in fact reality. In the days of the Cold War there was more talk about the non-existent Iron Curtain than about the Berlin Wall.

P.L.T.: The animals of your *Grande Parade* are a direct reference to the Little People of folklore?

A.A.: They appear very humble, and maybe they are. I've often heard about the sacredness of animals and their innocence. But what about their humility? Nevertheless, they file by with sticks of dynamite taped on their backs.
The animals ask, "Are you ready for this circus? Are you ready for the next fireworks? Are you ready for the next series of explosions?"
For my part, I keep to my cave and I receive images from the outside world which I draw afterwards. It's warm and comfortable here. Fernand Léger lived in a different world. That world is finished, in the same way that the hopes of those times wilted long ago. Erik Satie, Jean Cocteau, Serge Diaghilev, Pablo Picasso, Francis Picabia are gone, their parade too.
The procession of my "Little People" will take place in great pomp. And to the spectator, these drawings declare: "I know what you're thinking about, you've got to change your life."
P.L.T.: Once again in praise of the minority?
A.A.: For the video *Mémoire*, which I just finished, I wanted to have a chimpanzee write. But since it is forbidden to work with chimpanzees in the United States, I filmed a baboon. It's almost impossible for monkeys to write... So it placed the letters—"TUTSI," "HUTU"—in a playful and sublime manner.
Here, it's even less than a minority, it's a different species. Before man, *Homo sapiens*, in a primordial state. Without what we call human dignity. *Mémoire* expresses responsibility for me. To say responsibility is also to say guilt. To

quote Dostoevsky in *The Brothers Karamazov*: "We are all guilty for all, before all, and I more than the others."

I imagine myself giving this baboon a voice.

What each of us hears, sees, feels to a very high degree remains engraved, printed in memory. I happened to be in the wrong place at the wrong time. I didn't know what was going on, and this ignorance was terrible: Even worse, nothing seemed really wrong in my eyes. And from there comes the fact that my knowledge doesn't apply to what is good or bad, but only to pleasure and pain. The experience was both strange and terrifying. But there I was: I heard, saw, felt. It remained etched in my memory.

What's left in me is a feeling of waste, sadness, senselessness.

But you, the spectators, you may know what all this means. And so you will become the messengers of this testimony.

Above all, don't forget: this is only a performance. For you, for your entertainment.

P.L.T.: But that's also the voice of the artist, between mute monkey and higher consciousness.

A.A.: I don't know why, when there's suffering, we start talking about animals.

In the photo *Séparation*, where I'm shown about to hug a lion, I raised the question: where does this separation come from? This break between man and animals?

Concerning this caricature of man being superior to animals, I'd say: To each his own. To avoid the lie that consists in saying: "love animals and hate man," I would like to express my feeling that man can be sublime.

If I remember right, Van Gogh wrote to [his brother] Theo that he wanted to turn lies into reality, with more truth.

P.L.T.: Truth keeps coming back in your talk. What is the relationship between reality and truth for you? In today's culture, we often talk of *reality*, using the English word. On the contrary, very little of truth. Even among the intellectuals and scientists of our time.

A.A.: We have reached a point where we can say that the situation of reality is to remain out of sight and out of mind.

P.L.T.: What do you mean?

Between Caravaggio's realism and today's reality shows, not to forget the realism of Soviet art, is there really a difference apart from the quality—very high in the former, very trivial in the others?

Isn't it the same model of a means of ideological persuasion?

A.A.: The only reality that matters is the cry. "Father, Father, why have you abandoned me?"; these are the words that Christ spoke in his death throes, nailed to his Cross. These are not words of hope, but of despair, without an answer. In dying, god becomes man, and fulfils his destiny. I multiplied with barbed wire to the point of decorativeness the body of the Crucified as painted by Grünewald; bristling with thorns, he is nothing but one huge wound. The wound of a razor blade... The thing that wounds becomes the material for the representation of the wounded. Reproduced four times, he is no more than an ordinary mortal, like Christ who died on Golgotha, lost in the midst of thieves and murderers.

P.L.T.: So reality always manifests itself for you in despair and wounds? Isn't there a happy, healthy, positive reality?

A.A.: Today's reality is sick with violence, misery, the exodus that it generates. If you don't want to die with it, the only possible way out is creativity. Deep inside me, despair. And inside despair, the strength to create...

P.L.T.: Reality would therefore be the last horizon of the misfortune of contemporary consciousness, at the same time as the source, the origin of all creation?

A.A.: We have to learn to look at art in the same way as human existence. In our everyday life, we have to get rid of everything that's unpleasant and negative; and passionately search for the poetic.

P.L.T.: To live art in the same way as life. To love life in the same way as art.

A.A.: I compare art with diving. When you're underwater and have a problem, to get out of your difficulty, you have to go back to the surface—as I already said, reality is violent. But nothing comes of being aggressive, because the pressure is much too high. In a way, art and life are the same.

The difference is that, if you want to contemplate art, most of the time you have to buy a ticket to look at a certain work or attend a concert...

P.L.T.: Life itself isn't free either.

A.A.: I prefer talking about a dream, a verse of poetry, a drawing, or an experience. The connection between life and image, between the drawing and a pair of boots, is existence...

The boots belong to no one, they're suspended between presence and absence, the presence of the drawing and the absence of a direct reference of some kind. They're the object of a drawing, suspended between the space of meanings and that of substance.

Van Gogh painted a pair of shoes in 1886. Picasso admired this painting and, in the 1930s, Martin Heidegger used it as an example in a series of lectures and even published an article on it in 1950. For Heidegger, the artist was the origin of the work of art, the work of art the source of the artist. Taking Van Gogh's shoes as an example, the German philosopher maintained that the very essence of a work of art consisted in the mere revelation of being.

My drawing of boots points back to this story and doesn't lead anywhere.

He says that life is the result of our actions and our capacity to produce images.

In the exhibition that I did at David Zwirner in New York, there was this perfect drawing hanging in one room, between the space of signs and the space of substance.

P.L.T.: Could you be more exact about what you mean with space of signs and space of substance?

A.A.: I already told you, Pier Luigi, that all works are autobiographical.
One day, I saw my daughters watching *Three Little Pigs*, as scared as if night were falling.
That led me to appropriate this music, brutally and violently. I always appropriate knowledge, the intellectual, the beauty of this world in a brutal manner.
The song's message compelled me to act.
I began to look into it.
It was in 1933, the folksong *Who's Afraid of the Big Bad Wolf?* was hummed by the Fiddler Pig and the Fifer Pig when they arrogantly thought that their straw and wooden houses would protect them from the Big Bad Wolf.
One of my daughters asked me: "Daddy, do you think that animals like music?"
—"Yes, of course!"
I see Nietzsche fainting while a horse is being beaten.

P.L.T.: What were you thinking about when you prepared this exhibition?

A.A.: A few years before his death, Barnett Newman painted *Who's Afraid of Red, Yellow and Blue?* in 1966, during the Cold War, some years after the Cuban missile crisis and in the middle of the Vietnam War.
David Zwirner talked to me about taxidermied animals and he said that the customs regulations for transporting them from Europe to the United States were different. Finally, he asked if this work was supposed to travel. The most important thing is to know the size of the doors.

Who's afraid of the big bad wolf?

That was the title of my exhibition, which had two main parts.

I began with the gallery on the right, the space of Signs: the first work was *La Grande Parade*, a series of drawings that covered the walls of the rooms, like paintings in the Lascaux or Tassili caverns. For me, they are the first sign. We call them "paintings," but in fact they are "drawings." Of course these "Little People," these modern kamikazes, with their parading, also recall Fernand Léger's title. The second proof referred to the second sign, the historic, prime sign, the cry: the cry of Christ, the cry transfigured by Grünewald, which I take up again in *Décor*.

The third sign is still to come, it's still unknown. That's the diagnosis of Jacques Derrida, from whom I took the title for this work. "The future belongs to ghosts," he said. From Adolf Hitler to Barack Obama, a forest of microphones carries words into the world, *urbi et orbi*, without any indulgence. Soon they will be transparent before disappearing forever in the bottomless pits of the history of the future. Ghosts. The apparent and ephemeral transparency of ghosts.

Derrida... The transparency of glass is not a virtue, it's a material quality.

P.L.T.: So the space was divided into two distinct parts. Signs on the one side and Substance on the other?

A.A.: Substance is also a Sign—but it is above all Substance, it belongs to matter. In the gallery on the left, the space of Substance, there were four works.

In the first room, *Hope*: an abandoned boat. A stranded hope. Boats stranded on the coasts of the world. Monuments to hope. Was the hope ruined during the passage from a sad yet loved homeland and the promising and distant horizon of a probed paradise where all ills would be healed?

The boat was taken from the real world: it really accompanied travelers to the American coast, from Cuba to Florida, where it was found. And then it was beached. It is what it's supposed to be, what it became after an ill-fated journey. Henceforth it is filled with garbage bags. The garbage bags are made of resin: they're sculptures. They say that these boats carry debris, the scum of the earth. They say that in different languages and different tones of voice. As an artist, I use my language: I make resin sculptures in the shape of garbage bags. To each his voice. From the glaciers of Caspar David Friedrich to the Mediterranean, to the Gulf of Mexico, to the East Indian Ocean, they are the wrecks of an odyssey or tsunami.

The shipwreck of Caspar David Friedrich is called *Hoffnung*, and I don't like the word, because we don't need hope, we need truth.

In the second room, three works.

Coup de tête: a sculpture, the monument to defeat. Zidane seems to dominate it, but at the same time, in this brief moment of dominance, he becomes the real loser. One day, my mother told me: "When I see Zidane, it makes me think of your childhood, and what I could have missed out on..."

Who's afraid of the big bad wolf? is a "painting" of burned animals of the same size as Picasso's *Guernica*. They never had a right to speak up, these burned animals. Yet we recognize them, they have a substance, a reality. What's left of them has undergone several operations: death, taxidermy, fire. Henceforth they are packed together in a shapeless mass of charred hides and other materials. Who's still afraid of them? Who's afraid of their still menacing presence, when, alive, they share with us the world in which we live? It was in 1933 that the song *Who's Afraid of the Big Bad Wolf?* was presented for the first time in a Walt Disney cartoon, *Three Little Pigs*. In 1933, Adolf Hitler was democratically elected chancellor of Germany. It was in 1937 that the Basque city of Guernica was bombed by German and Italian aircraft, killing more than a quarter of the population, and Picasso executed a monumental painting in memory of it.

P.L.T.: There was one last work in this room, a video titled *Mémoire*, which you already talked about. What part did it play in the whole?

A.A.: The monkey, by placing the letters that compose the names "HUTU" and "TUTSI" makes a dull sound, like a metronome. The sound of memory: the blows of an ax, for a genocide with machetes.

P.L.T.: In between the two rooms, there was a

drawing of boots. What were they doing there?
A.A.: It was simply the way that led nowhere. Hence the presence of this work which we already talked about: *Chemins qui ne mènent nulle part.*
P.L.T.: Don't the paths lead to Beaubourg [Centre Georges Pompidou]?
A.A.: Of course. But there, that'll be something else. I'm working with Philippe-Alain Michaud on creating a sort of mental landscape between inside and outside, plus a passage through the entrance hall. I'd like to take inside, into the museum, what originally occupied the margins and periphery: for example, *Practice ZERO TOLERANCE.*
One day, by chance, a speech by Bush and Sarkozy was being announced on TV. At the same instant, my eyes fell on a sentence by Woody Allen: "The answer is yes, but could you remind me of the question..." My daughters were horsing around and Elle, my second daughter, turned the TV off. That's my infernal daughter who can't keep her hands off anything. I turned the set back on and heard the words "zero tolerance." It was scary. I always thought that contemporary capitalist societies were built on extreme molds. Practicing zero tolerance is making a mold, filling it with clay, taking the mold away and firing it in a kiln.
In the intermediate passage between the atrium at the entrance, between inside and outside, the mass of *Telle mère tel fils*, this sort of vision, hallucinatory in its material and sensual realism. And finally, outside, *Coup de tête*, faith as pres-

ence and monument at the same time.

P.L.T.: And so someone came down from the mountain of elsewhere like the ancient prophets of truth and walked into the *beau bourg* of the museum institution—conservative like all institutions—bore witness to the conflicts and discord, and proclaimed words of change and transformation.

A.A.: It is time it came time. It is time.

Paris, March 2012
Translated by Jean-Marie Clarke

Works

CHEMINS QUI NE MÈNENT NULLE PART, 2011, CHARCOAL ON PAPER,
47 5/8 x 31 1/2 INCHES (121 x 80 CM), PRIVATE COLLECTION.

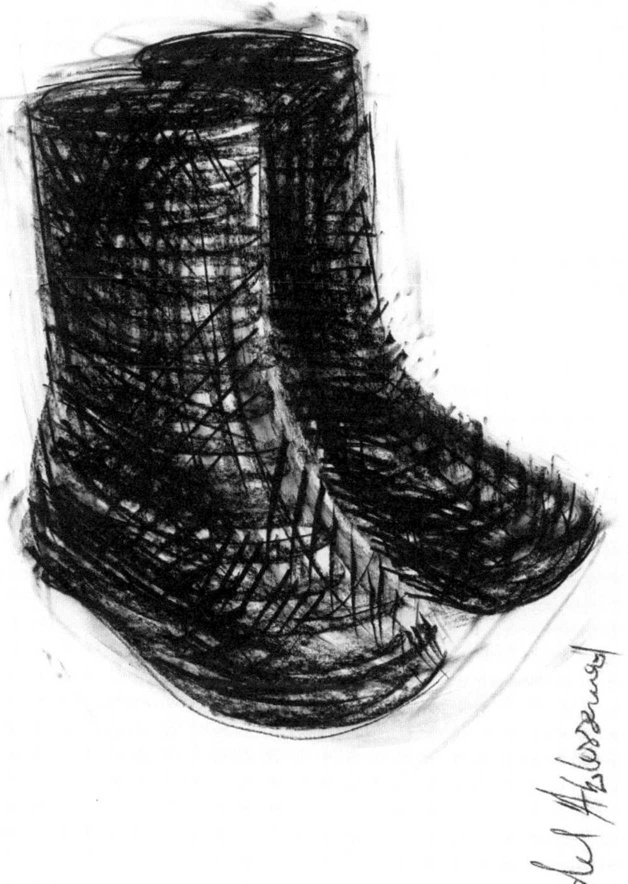

LA GRANDE PARADE (DETAIL), 2011-2012, CHARCOAL ON PAPER,
40 DRAWINGS, DIMENSIONS VARY FROM 23 1/2 x 31 1/2 INCHES
(59.8 x 80 CM) – 64 3/4 x 82 1/5 INCHES (164.5 x 208.8 CM),
ABOVE: 31 4/5 x 47 1/4 INCHES (79.8 x 120 CM), PRIVATE COLLECTION.

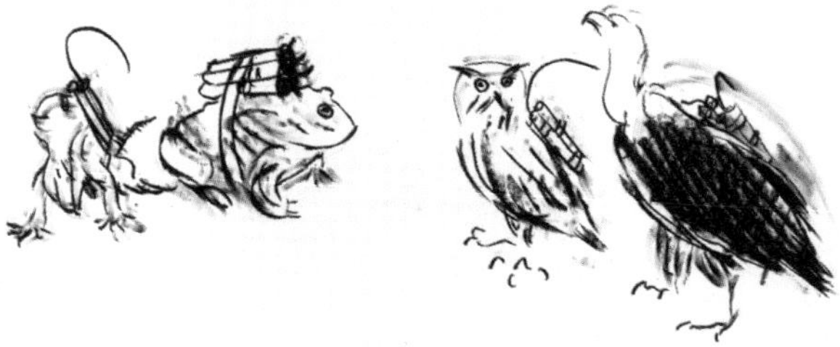

WHO'S AFRAID OF THE BIG BAD WOLF? (DETAIL), 2011-2012,
TAXIDERMY, STEEL, AND WIRE, 143 x 307 INCHES (363.2 x 779.8 CM),
COLLECTION OF THE ARTIST.

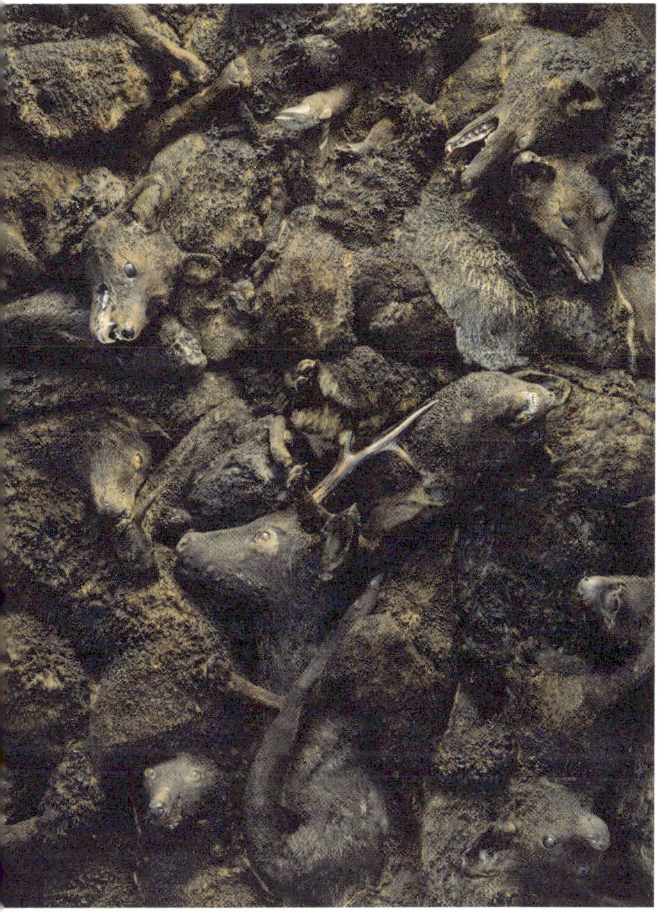

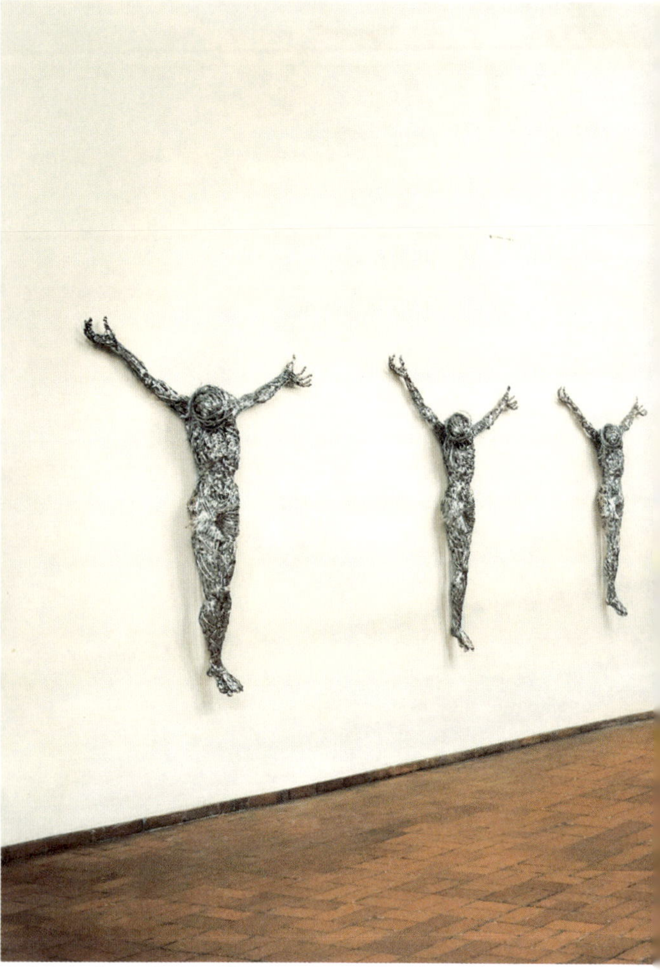

DÉCOR, 2011-2012, RAZOR WIRE, 4 ELEMENTS,
EACH APPROXIMATELY: 82 5/8 x 68 1/2 x 16 1/8 INCHES (210 x 174 x 41 CM),
COLLECTION FRANÇOIS PINAULT.
Installation view at Musée Unterlinden, Colmar, 2012, facing the Isenheim Altarpiece by Matthias Grünewald and Nicolas de Haguenau, between 1512-1516.

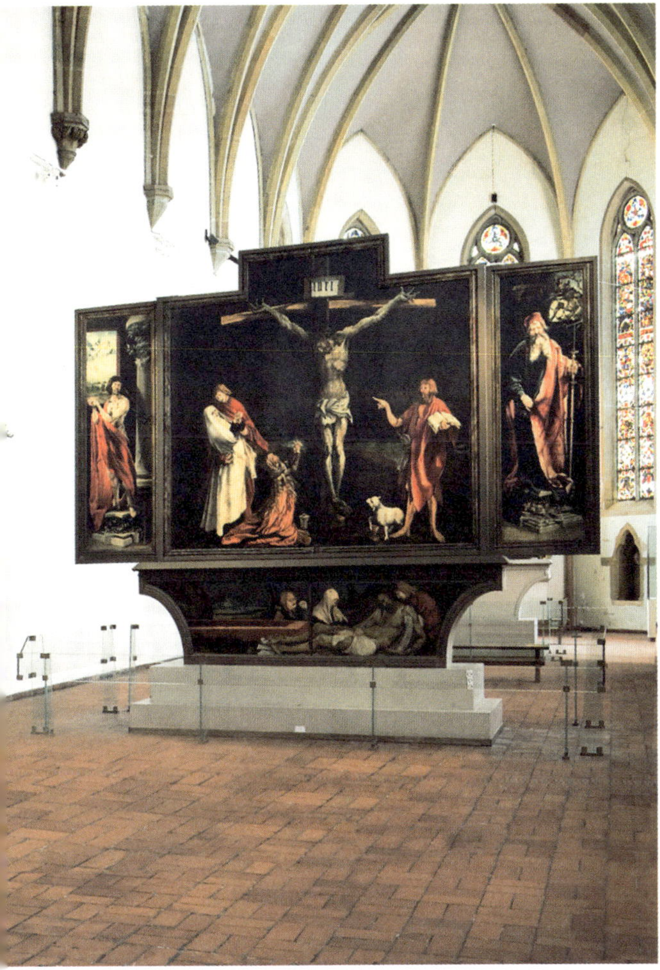

GOD IS DESIGN, 2005, VIDEO ANIMATION, 4 MIN 6 SEC (LOOP),
BLACK AND WHITE, SOUND, 3050 DRAWINGS, DIMENSIONS VARY.
Installation view of "Universal Code: Art and Cosmology in the Information Age,"
The Power Plant, Toronto, Canada, 2009.

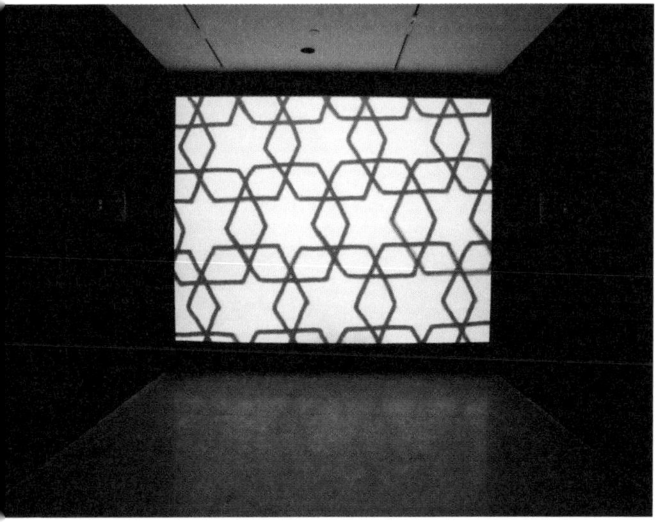

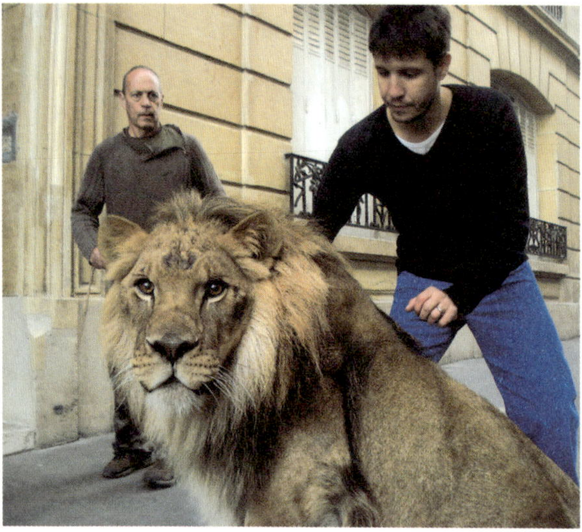

SÉPARATION, 2006, INKJET PRINT, 35 2/5 x 40 1/2 INCHES (90 x 103 CM).

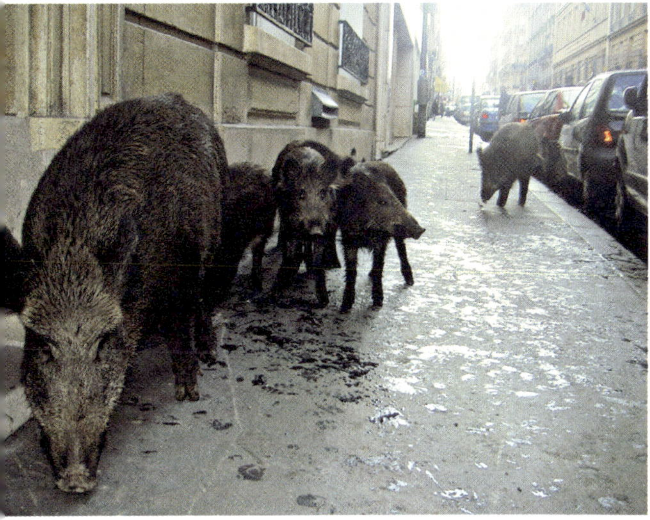

SEPT FRÈRES, 2006, INKJET PRINT, 29 1/8 x 39 3/8 INCHES (74 x 100 CM).

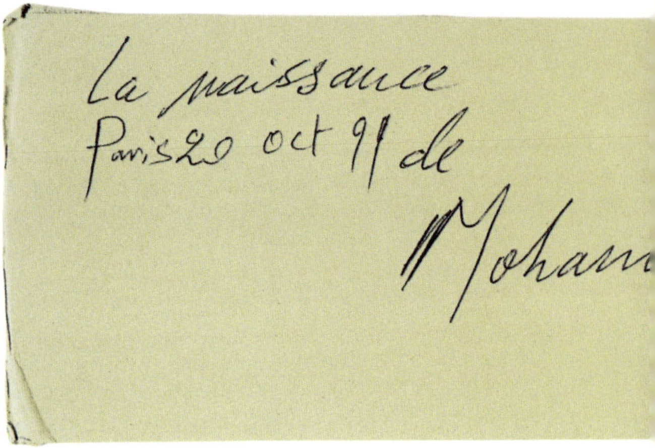

LA NAISSANCE DE MOHAMMEDKARLPOLPOT, 1999,
BALLPOINT PEN ON PAPER, 3 1/3 x 11 2/5 INCHES (8.5 x 29 CM),
COLLECTION OF THE ARTIST.

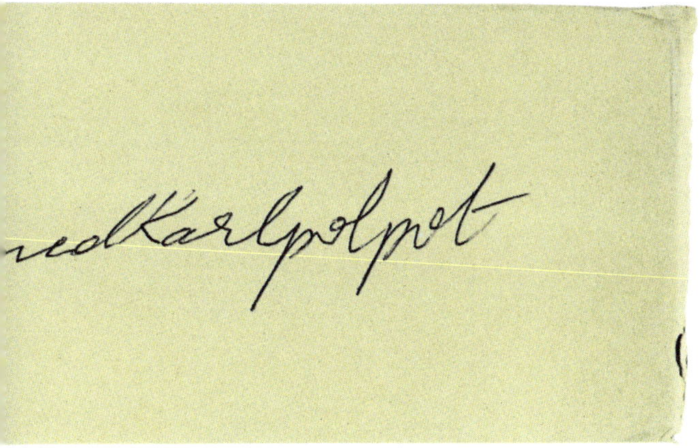

ZEN, 2000, VIDEO PROJECTION, 1 MIN 33 SEC (LOOP), COLOR, SOUND, DIMENSIONS VARY.

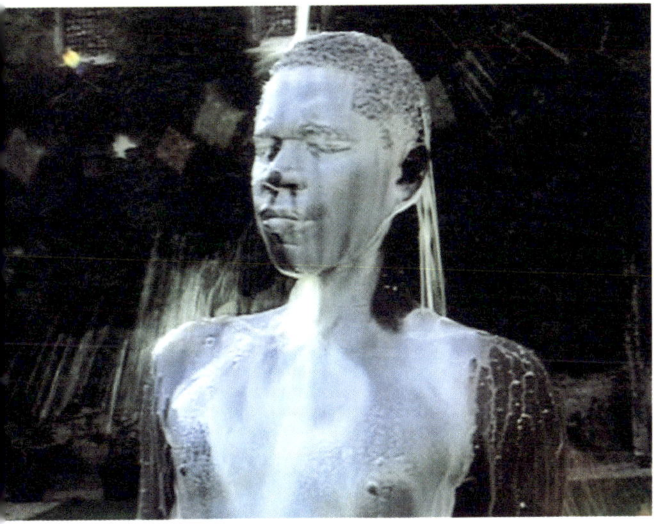

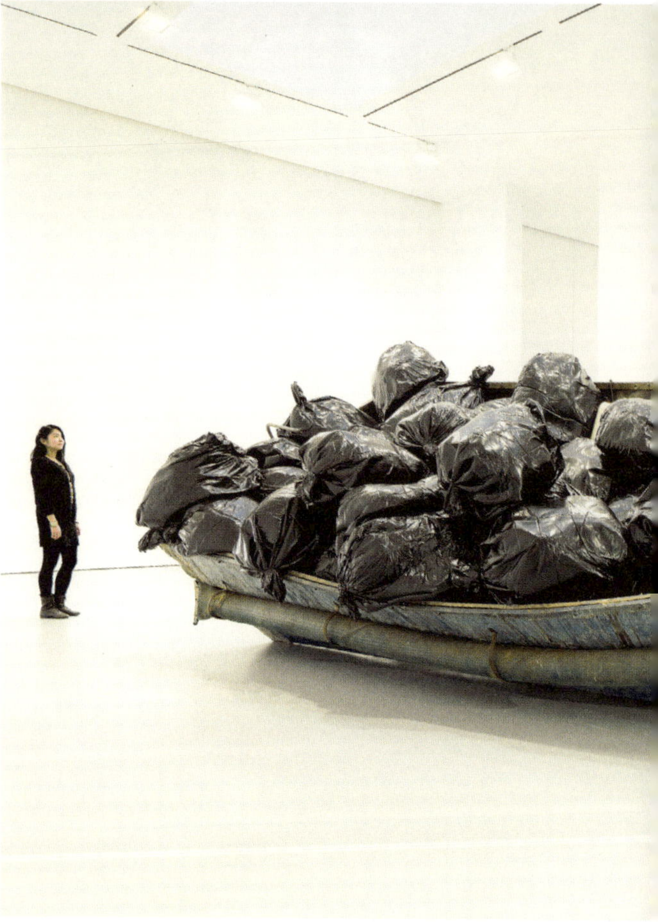

HOPE, 2011-2012, FOUND BOAT AND RESIN, 81 x 96 x 228 INCHES (205.7 x 243.8 x 579.1 CM).
Installation view of "Adel Abdessemed: Who's afraid of the big bad wolf ?," David Zwirner, New York, 2012.

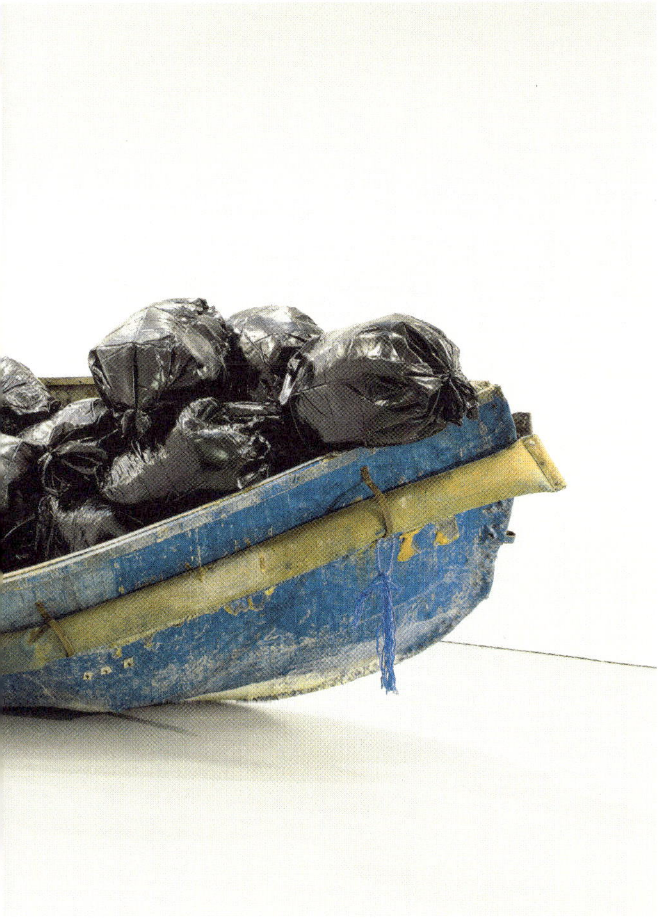

JOUEUR DE FLÛTE, 1996, VIDEO PROJECTION, 30 MIN 10 SEC (LOOP), COLOR, SOUND, DIMENSIONS VARY.

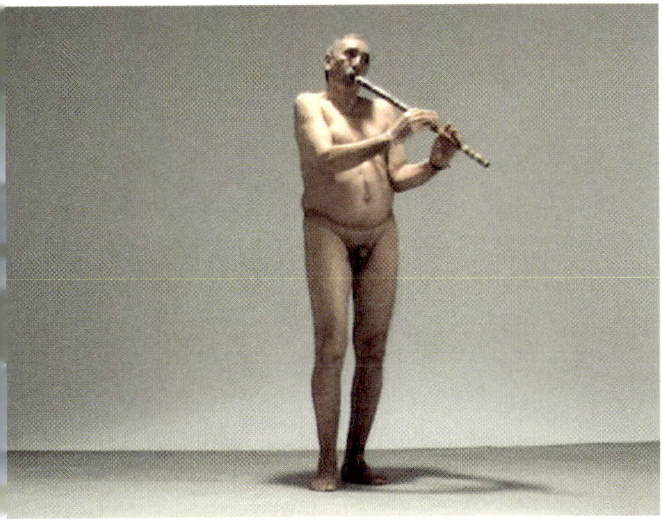

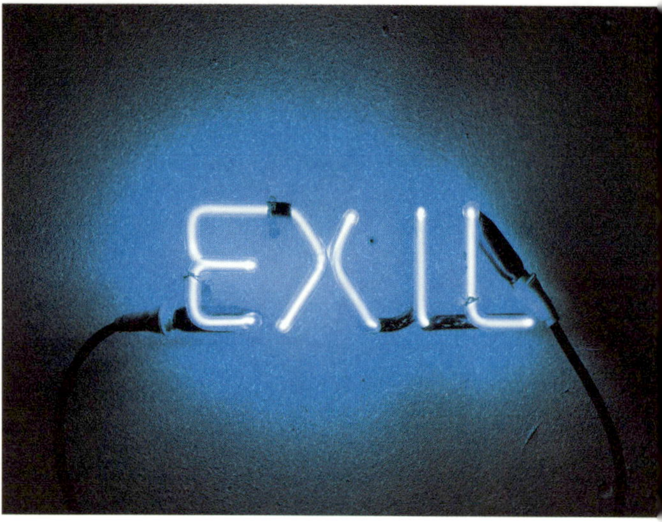

EXIT, 1996, BLUE NEON, 4 1/3 x 10 1/4 INCHES (11 x 26 CM).

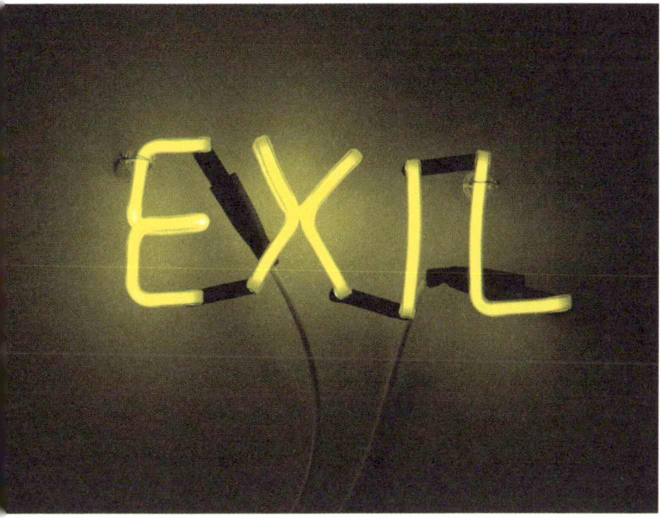

 EXIT, 2007, 9 YELLOW NEONS, EACH: 9 1/4 x 13 3/4 INCHES (23.5 x 34.9 CM), DETAIL.

PRACTICE ZERO TOLERANCE, 2006, TERRACOTTA,
173 2/5 x 55 1/8 x 55 1/8 INCHES (440 x 140 x 140 CM),
COLLECTION FRANÇOIS PINAULT.
Installation view of "In Praise of Doubt," Punta della Dogana, Venice, 2011.

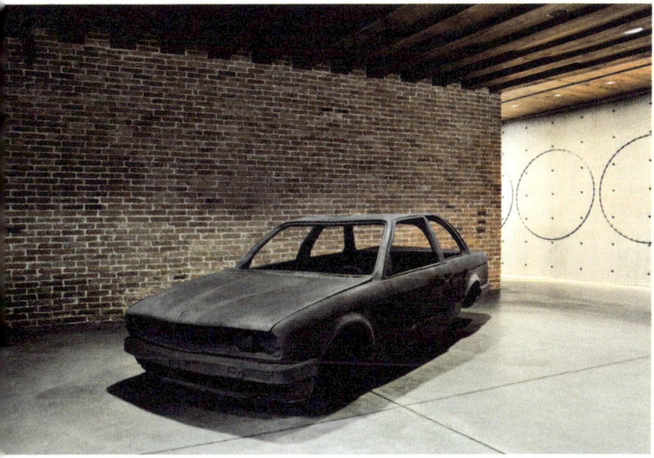

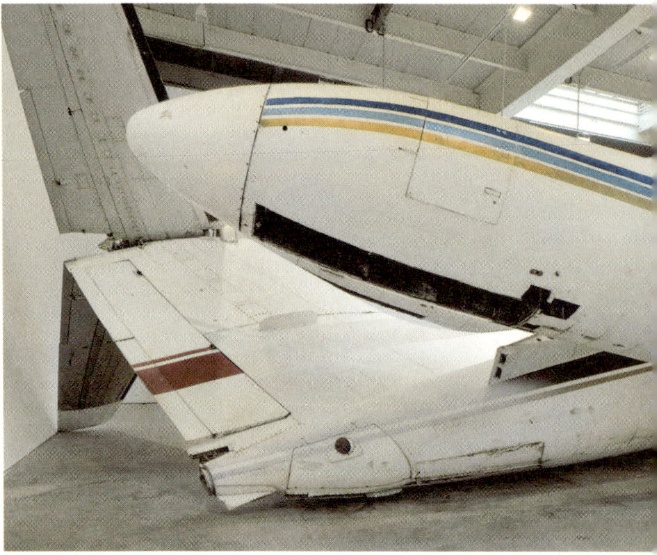

TELLE MÈRE TEL FILS, 2008, AIRPLANES, FELT, ALUMINUM, METAL,
88.6 x 13.1 x 16.4 FEET (27 x 4 x 5 M), COLLECTION BUDI TEK.
Installation view of "Adel Abdessemed: RIO," David Zwirner, New York, 2009.

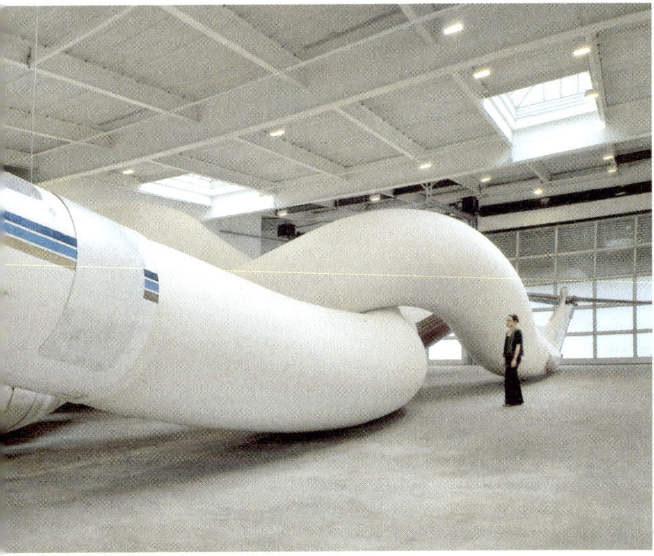

BOUREK, 2005, AEROJET COMMANDER PLANE FUSELAGE,
89 x 107 7/8 INCHES (226 x 274 CM), PRIVATE COLLECTION.
Installation view of "Adel Abdessemed: Dead or Alive,"
P.S.1 Contemporary Art Center, Long Island City, New York, 2007.

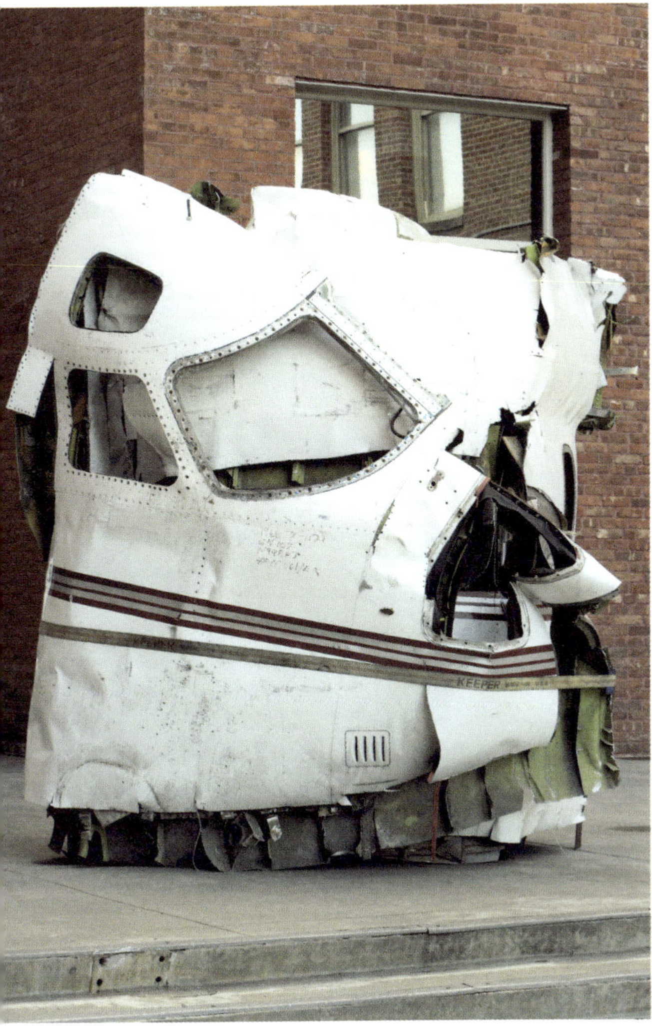
KEEPER

COUP DE TÊTE, 2012, RESIN, 88 1/2 x 62 x 37 1/2 INCHES
(224.8 x 157.5 x 95.3 CM).
Installation view of "Adel Abdessemed: Who's afraid of the big bad wolf ?,"
David Zwirner, New York, 2012.

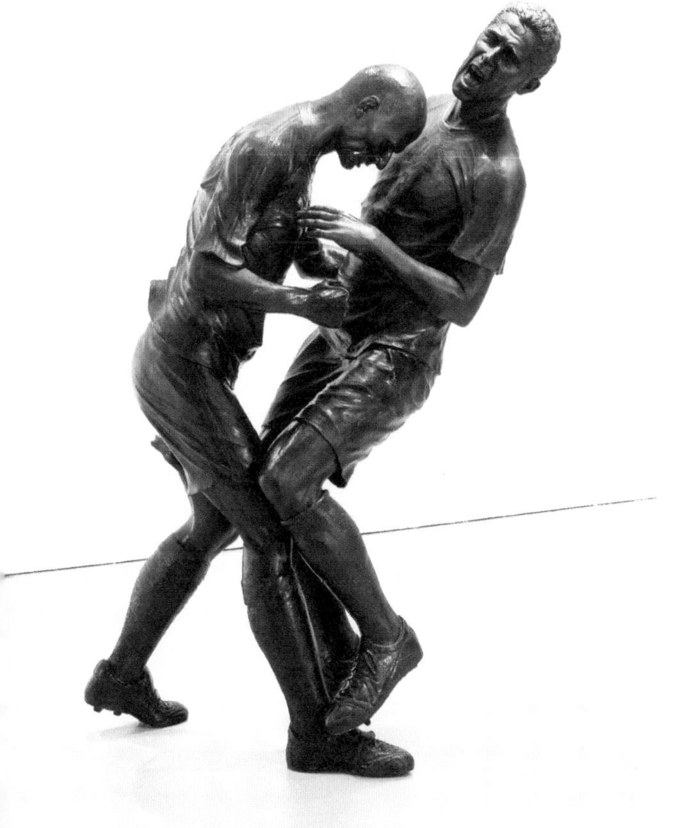

The Way Elsewhere

Donatien Grau

One of the fundamental features of any lively and intense interaction between two human beings is that it always leads elsewhere. Discussing one topic leads to addressing another, according to a succession that is loose by definition. Each goal that is reached becomes a new starting point, and the chain of these double laps constitutes the order of speech.

However, such an interaction is not just a flow of words and a dialogue between two persons. In the Ancient tradition, especially in the Stoicism of Seneca and Epictetus, such interactions, when organized, became a conversation, and then a discourse. It would be possible to summarize the tension between conversation and discourse around a resolution of the seeming opposition between the "order of speech," as verbal content, and the "order of discourse," in Michel Foucault's sense; that is, the theoretical and political organization of the discursive entity.

This difference must also be assumed from the situation of the discourse: who is talking? With whom is one talking? And last, but not least: about what? That being established, it would be possible to summarize the stakes in a single question: that of the topics of the discourse. In a conversation, even if there can be an agreement, or even complicity and friendship, each person knows his place: but two people engage in the process of having a conversation. "Con-versing", in Latin, means turning the one to the other. And this is exactly what a conversation such as this is about.

Of course, if the conversation is too hierarchic, if there is a relationship of dominance between the two parties, the purpose will certainly not be achieved. On the other hand, if the affinity is too great, if there is too much closeness, the construction of meaning will sometimes be lost for the sake of an ethics of restricted community from which the reader will be excluded by definition.

The art of *conversation* is therefore not an easy matter, and he who engages in it has the choice either of a naivety that both immunizes and anaesthetizes, or of a methodological questioning that often leads nowhere. One of the most real achievements of *Conversation* resides in the rigorous and playful maintenance of this tension. Adel Abdessemed and Pier Luigi Tazzi have known each other for more than a decade, they are tied by a deep mutual affection. The way of words leads somewhere. And this somewhere is elsewhere.

In company like this, Abdessemed does not hold back. In his work, of course, but also—and especially here—in *Conversation,* there is a refusal to be imprisoned in a context, be it geographical, intellectual, or personal. His references are manifold, but they never amount to decoration or an illustrative presence. Each one has come to inhabit the mind and heart of a man who, mornings, before sunrise, spends several hours plunged in his books. It is because everything that has to matter matters that he would not accept the possibility of being imprisoned.

This *Conversation* in the present publication is surely a document of great value: a living sign of the vision that an artist nurtures of the world and of his positioning of himself face to face with it, in revolt against it, in a deeper harmony with the inspiration that constitutes it. As such, it is much more as well: this book, which Abdessemed likes to qualify as a "book of affirmations," crystallizes the effort of movement. The way not only leads elsewhere, in the sense that the problems come and go in the flow of dialogue. It also leads to an elsewhere which is that of art. When the artist describes a work, it is not the object that he evokes: it is a vision of worlds. When he talks, it is not the words of the everyday language that he uses: he refreshes and recasts their meaning. The reader of *Conversation* is rightly struck by the poetic tonality that pervades it. This is not a trivial fact: poetry, in modernism, is the language of revolution, of emigration elsewhere. When we opened this book, we thought that we were going elsewhere,

and we find ourselves converted to the necessity of experiencing an elsewhere that is art.
The imperative is explicit and categorical: "You have to change your life." The goal pursued by the artist, if it manifests an acute awareness of the necessity of something beyond everyday life, should not be thought of outside the world. On the contrary, in the time spent on the conversation, in the affirmation of his life values, Abdessemed reminds all of us who may have forgotten it that the experience of transcendence, when fully lived, is lived within the world. In so doing, he provides the reader with a wonderful lesson in immanent humanism.

Translated by Jean-Marie Clarke

Photography credits

Acknowledgments

The authors wish to thank:
Julie Abdessemed, Marie Andrasch, Aïté Bresson, Jean-Paul Capitani, Angelo Careri, Giovanni Careri, Jean-Marie Clarke, Donatien Grau, Lise Guéhenneux, Philippe-Alain Michaud, Françoise Nyssen, Raphaëlle Pinoncély, Anuwat Rattanaphan, Lisa Rey-Galiay, Paul Rondin, Lapo Ruggeri.
Véronique Ansorge, Anna Drozda, Julia Joern, and Louise Sørensen at David Zwirner gallery.
And in particular Angela Mengoni, who so generously made herself available to be the first reader of the text, and for having shared her sensitive comments with us.

Printed in August 2012 by Deux-Ponts,
on behalf of Actes Sud,
le Méjan, place Nina-Berberova, 13200 Arles
Registration of copyright
1st edition: September 2012